The Complete Guide to

Hiring and Firing Government Employees

The
Complete Guide
to
Hiring and Firing
Government Employees

Stewart Liff

AMACOM

American Management Association

New York • Atlanta • Brussels • Chicago • Mexico City • San Francisco
Shanghai • Tokyo • Toronto • Washington, D. C.

Special discounts on bulk quantities of AMACOM books are available to corporations, professional associations, and other organizations. For details, contact Special Sales Department, AMACOM, a division of American Management Association, 1601 Broadway, New York, NY 10019.
Tel: 800-250-5308. Fax: 518-891-2372.
E-mail: specialsls@amanet.org
Website: www.amacombooks.org/go/specialsales
To view all AMACOM titles go to: www.amacombooks.org

This publication is designed to provide accurate and authoritative information in regard to the subject matter covered. It is sold with the understanding that the publisher is not engaged in rendering legal, accounting, or other professional service. If legal advice or other expert assistance is required, the services of a competent professional person should be sought.

Library of Congress Cataloging-in-Publication Data

Liff, Stewart.
  The complete guide to hiring and firing government employees / Stewart Liff
     p. cm.
  Includes bibliographical references and index.
  ISBN-13: 978-0-8144-1450-7
  ISBN-10: 0-8144-1450-8
  1. United States—Officials and employees—Selection and appointment. 2. United States—Officials and employees—Dismissal of. I. Title.

  JK731.L54 2010
  352.6'50973—dc22

                                        2009031624

Printing number

10 9 8 7 6 5 4 3 2 1

This book is dedicated to my wife, Lisa,

who is my best friend in the world.

Contents

INTRODUCTION

THIS BOOK WAS WRITTEN to address two of the most important issues that government managers will ever have to face: how to hire and fire a government employee. Neither of these is easy, but in all probability, you will need to do both in order to succeed.

Most likely, you will hire far more employees than you will fire—if not, something is definitely wrong. After all, if you spend most of your time correcting bad hiring decisions, what does that say about your hiring process? Moreover, you will find yourself devoting far too much of your precious time looking for ways to get rid of bad employees instead of performing your day-to-day job responsibilities.

In the course of a long career, you may hire dozens if not hundreds of people, and make no mistake about it, the quality of the people you hire will go a long way toward determining how successful you are as a manager. Unfortunately, in my experience, government managers often spend an inordinate amount of time bringing in large groups of new hires without devoting enough time to strategizing *how to bring in the best possible group of new employees.* As a result, these managers find themselves hiring a mix of candidates, many of whom prove to be less than optimal selections. Eventually, the managers wind up scrambling to try and deal with the problems inherent in a weak workforce. These problems range from a wide variety of training challenges to employee relations issues to performance problems, many of which could have been avoided had managers taken more time to plan properly and had they possessed the skills needed to hire an excellent group of new employees in the first place.

That is not to say that it is easy to hire top-notch government employees. It most certainly is not. The government's laws, rules, regulations, and procedures for hiring, regardless of whether it's at the federal, state, or local levels, are for the most part complex, convoluted, time-consuming, and in many cases highly frustrating—to both government managers and the people trying to get jobs with the government. In addition, the requirements of factoring in veterans' preference, the legitimate concerns about equal employment opportunities (EEO) for all, competition from the private sector (which can hire more quickly and doesn't have the same procedures as the government), centralized pressure to hire quickly when recruitment authority is granted, unanticipated budget crunches, rigid pay systems, hiring freezes, and others all make the hiring process challenging for government managers.

According to the United States Merit Systems Protection Board (MSPB), which serves as an independent, bipartisan guardian of the merit systems under which federal employees work, "There are barriers to recruiting a high quality workforce. . . . First-line supervisors and other managers still indicate that they have problems recruiting highly qualified applicants. These problems may be due to insufficient recruitment strategies or incentives, the slowness of the hiring process, or the use of inadequate measuring instruments, and agencies should examine them further."[1]

That being said, government managers can take many steps to enable themselves to hire excellent employees, and that is part of the basis for this book. Having been a government employee for more than 32 years, and a government manager and leader for 28 years, I know firsthand what it is like to try and hire employees within the constraints that exist. Moreover, during nearly my entire career, I have hired people while working in high-cost areas such as New York City, Los Angeles, and Washington D.C., which only made the challenge even greater.

The first half of this book is devoted to showing readers how to hire excellent government employees in a logical, integrated, and comprehensive fashion. It is intended to be a road map for hiring quality people within a government personnel system, regardless of the level of government. It is based on both my experiences as a government human resources management (HRM) expert and my many years as a government line manager and senior executive.

This book is not meant to provide a "one-design-fits-all" approach to recruitment. Rather, it offers a series of philosophies, strategies, and recruitment tactics based on a deep understanding of the government's HRM systems and many years of working in the real world of government staffing and line management that can then be customized to a specific, local situation.

The book is also designed to help you look at your entire process, ranging from the time before vacancies even exist to the moment you begin your recruitment process through rating and ranking candidates and up to the final selection process and its aftermath. I am confident that if you adopt this holistic approach, it will greatly aid you in building a first-class government workforce—and preclude you from having to deal with too many poor-quality employees down the road.

While building your workforce, it is quite likely that you are going to find that one or more of your employees are simply not working out. They may be holdovers from the past who have never been good employees and have not been dealt with, they may be good employees whose performance has suffered due to personal problems or other reasons, or they may be recent hires who turned out to be poor selections despite your best efforts. Regardless of the reason, most organizations, including high-performing ones, have some poor performers. The difference is that *the best organizations deal with these employees, and the more marginal ones do not.* This seems to be especially true for government, given its myriad rules and culture, wherein far too many problem employees are allowed to coast through their jobs.

From my perspective, this happens because many, if not most, government managers have bought into the perception that you can't fire a bad employee. They believe that it is too difficult, too time-consuming, and too much work so they often give up before they even get started. Personal experience, or the lessons they have learned from others, has taught managers that there is no point in trying to remove a bad apple because in the end they will not prevail. So why go through all of the pain and suffering that the government's personnel system will impose on them?

The problem with this type of thinking is that it perpetuates the widespread belief that you can't fire a bad government employee. Once the public believes this myth, it undermines their faith in government. Once your employees believe this, it ruins their morale and makes them conclude that they are working for a less-than-stellar organization that is not interested in high performance. When your problem employees see that management is not prepared to deal with them, they will be emboldened to slack off even more and will try to influence marginal employees to take the same approach. In short, you will be encouraging a cancer to metastasize in your organization at a rapid rate.

This does not have to happen in government, nor should it. However, it has been happening for decades because government leaders have done a relatively poor job of building accountability into its personnel systems; leaders have not taught their subordinate supervisors why it is so important to deal with problem employees up front; and supervisors do not really know how to go about actually dealing with a poor employee.

According to the MSPB, "In many Federal organizations, there is a culture that sanctions not dealing effectively with problem employees. This must be changed for the Government to effectively hold employees accountable for their performance."[2]

Make no mistake about it, changing the culture is not an easy thing to do. The system is definitely complex and requires a high degree of technical knowledge, which most supervisors do not possess. Moreover, going through the process is not a pleasant experience because you will likely experience pushback from the affected employee(s), which may very well entail one or more complaints being filed against you. You may also get second-guessed or overturned by upper management at some point in the process, which will make your experience even more frustrating.

Herein lies the problem: How do we change the way that government operates so that its management officials recognize that it is in their best interest to deal with their problem employees? According to an MSPB report,

> . . . despite the claims of some supervisors to the contrary, we believe that the current system can provide the means to deal with problem employees. This does not imply that changes to the current system should not be considered; it only implies that managers should not wait for systemic adjustments before they take appropriate action in this area. The current system does not, of course, make the process of

dealing with problem employees a particularly pleasant experience. Nor does the system work well unless management creates an organizational climate that makes it clear to all employees that poor performance or misconduct will not be tolerated.³

I fully agree with that conclusion, which, by the way, was reached about 10 years ago. Since the time that MSPB report was issued, there have been no significant changes to the system. The key continues to be to change the mind-set of government managers by showing them the way and providing them with the skills necessary to deal with poor employees, which includes firing employees when necessary.

That is the purpose of the second part of this book: to teach readers how to successfully terminate poor employees within the system that currently exists. When appropriate, it should be and can be done.

Before I continue, let me be clear about one thing: You should fire a government employee only as a last resort and only when it is the right thing to do. Never fire someone because it is expedient or because you are trying to show that you are a "tough guy." Only take this step when it is appropriate and will promote the efficiency of the government. Remember, your organization has already invested an enormous amount of time, energy, and money in the employee, so you should fire the person only when there is no other reasonable alternative.

Please note that I do not consider a reasonable alternative to be moving a problem employee from one team to another without addressing the root cause. Otherwise you are merely perpetuating the problem, creating headaches for the employee's new supervisor, and sending a message to the rest of the workforce that you are not serious about dealing with difficult employees.

Also, I do not consider giving a well-known problem employee a "slap on the wrist" because that is not going to change his behavior either. As you will learn later on in this book, in order to successfully deal with a true problem employee, as opposed to a good employee whose conduct or performance problem is merely an aberration, you need to let the employee know that if he doesn't change his performance or behavior, you are prepared to remove him. That is the only way to let the employee know you are serious.

After all, when you are dealing with someone who is truly a problem (i.e., someone who is in the bottom 10 percent of your workforce), the only successful outcomes are to either change the person or *change* the person. The one outcome that is not acceptable is maintaining the status quo, wherein the employee continues to behave and act in an unacceptable manner. That must change; otherwise, the employee will surely pollute your workplace and other employees will conclude that management is sanctioning the employee's actions and that "what's good for the goose is good for the gander."

If there are no reasonable alternatives to firing the employee, and progressive discipline has not worked (more about that topic in Section 2: How to Fire a Government Employee), then by all means go forward and take action to remove the employee. This book will show you how to fire an employee in a fair, logical, and defensible manner. It will provide you with tips on how to go about it, including how to conduct an investigation, how to document your actions, how to write charges, how to put together an evidence file, how and when to settle a case, and, if not settlement, how to prevail before a third party. It will also demystify the process for you, so you will know what you are getting into, what the potential pitfalls are (and how to avoid them), and what to expect along the way.

SECTION

1

How to Hire a Government Employee

1

THE GOVERNMENT'S HIRING PROCESS

SIMPLY PUT, all government agencies try to hire the best candidates possible while using an open, fair, and equitable process. As nearly everyone knows, selections for government jobs are intended to be based on qualifications without regard to race, color, religion, gender, national origin, disability, age, or any other nonmerit factor.

However, the process itself, regardless of the level of government, has generally been slow, time-consuming, unwieldy, and frustrating for government employers, and overly complex, hard to understand, and difficult to navigate for potential employees. All in all, the systems in place have not pleased anyone, as they frequently have made it hard for government employers to hire the people they want in a timely manner, and, conversely, the systems have often caused prospective employees to give up their pursuit because they found the process so difficult.

Government employees tend to see things the same way. For example, in a recent survey, less than 50 percent of federal employees reported that their "work unit is able to recruit people with the right skills."[1]

So how do government employers go about hiring top-notch candidates in the most effective and efficient manner possible? The best way to do this is to first understand how and why the government's recruitment systems have evolved to their current states over time. Such insight will enable you to understand the reasoning behind the development of these systems, and thus help you use them to your advantage.

Let's take a look at the history of government recruitment, particularly at the federal level, so we can see how the process has evolved.

History

To a large extent, the civil service system that most of us are familiar with dates back to the Pendleton Civil Service Reform Act of 1883,[2] which among other things established the United States Civil Service Commission (today known as the U.S. Office of Personnel Management [OPM]) and placed most federal government employees on the merit system.

The Pendleton Act marked the end of the so-called "spoils system," which many people believe had started under President Andrew Jackson.

> A spoils system is an informal practice where a political party, after winning an election, gives government jobs to its voters as a reward for working toward victory, and as an incentive to keep working for the party—as opposed to a system of awarding offices on the basis of some measure of merit independent of political activity, or merit system. The term was derived from the phrase "to the victor go the spoils."[3]

In reality, it is hard to pinpoint exactly where and when the system started, but at the federal level, George Washington looked for civil service candidates who were honest and efficient, but he also employed an informal litmus test that gave preference to Federalists and, on occasion, to officers of the Revolutionary Army.

President John Adams took a relatively similar approach to Washington, but Adams was a bit more partisan in his appointments. Most notably, he made his so-called "midnight appointments," which he held during his final days in office. According to the OPM, "Knowing that he would be succeeded by a President of the opposition party, Adams attempted to obtain some control of the judicial branch of the new administration by appointing some

Federalists to circuit court judgeships and others to justice of the peace positions in the District of Columbia."[4]

President Thomas Jefferson, a Democratic-Republican, felt that he had to "redress the balance" by appointing only Democratic-Republicans until an equilibrium was attained between his party and the Federalist Party. Jefferson has been unjustifiably referenced as the first president to introduce partisan politics as a factor in removals and appointments. In fact, Jefferson wrote that his removals would be "as few as possible, done gradually, and bottomed on some malversation or inherent disqualification maintained a policy of preventing rival Federalists from attaining government offices and frequently reviewed lists of civil service and military officer appointments."[5]

Presidents James Madison and James Monroe both made appointments irrespective of party affiliation, which created a relative degree of peace and calm between our nation's political parties. However, the Tenure of Office Act of 1820 was passed during Monroe's term and it ultimately facilitated the establishment of the spoils system. The act limited the terms of many officials to four years, and eventually it led to the removal of all incumbents becoming nearly customary. It is important to emphasize that neither Monroe nor his successor, John Quincy Adams, took advantage of the act. However, President Adams quickly discovered that hiring for the civil service was no easy task:

> On such appointments all the wormwood and gall of the old party hatred ooze out. Not a vacancy to any office occurs but there is a distinguished Federalist started and pushed home as a candidate to fill it, always well qualified, sometimes in an eminent degree, and yet so obnoxious to the Republican party, that they cannot be appointed without exciting a vehement clamor against him and the administration. It becomes thus impossible to fill any vacancy in appointment without offending one half of the community.[6]

At the state level, successive New York governors in the early nineteenth century, most notably DeWitt Clinton, pioneered the spoils system.[7] Clinton filled offices with supporters, he drove out his enemies, and his "reputation for political hardball followed him even in death."[8]

After he became president in 1828, Andrew Jackson systematically rewarded his supporters. Jackson believed that the presidential election gave him a "mandate" to select his own people for key positions, and he argued that regular Americans could ably perform the duties formerly done by traditional civil service workers. Critics felt that such an approach made the civil service system vulnerable to corruption and incompetence, and that it was inconsistent with American principles.

Near the end of the Civil War, Congress passed the first significant piece of legislation granting preference to veterans. It provided that "Persons honorably discharged from the military or naval service by reason of disability resulting from wounds or sickness incurred in the line of duty shall be preferred for appointments to civil offices, provided they are found to possess the business capacity necessary for the proper discharge of the duties of such offices."[9]

Presidents following Andrew Jackson continued to use the spoils system. For example, Abraham Lincoln used it to support the Republican Party and further the war effort. However, national criticism of the spoils system continued, and after the Civil War ended, reformers began pushing for a formal civil service system. The rampant corruption that was prevalent under President Ulysses S. Grant only strengthened the push for change.

Drafted during the Chester A. Arthur administration, the Pendleton Act served as a response to President James Garfield's assassination by Charles Julius Guiteau, who thought he deserved a civil service ambassadorship after writing a speech in support of Garfield. The speech was given on, at most, two occasions, but Guiteau somehow believed that he played a major role in Garfield getting elected. He continually pressed for a job with the new administration, but he was rebuffed at every level, which eventually prompted him to murder the allegedly ungrateful president.

In order to subvert the spoils system's dangers, the act provided for some government jobs to be filled through written competitive examinations that were open to all citizens. In addition, it mandated that selections be made from the best qualified applicants without regard to political considerations.

After a series of party reversals at the presidential level, most federal jobs eventually came under the civil service.[10] Moreover, the rules were strengthened and required stricter compliance with the restrictions against political activity.[11] However, these laws applied to only federal jobs. They did not apply to the state and local jobs that were highly political in nature. Eventually, though, state and local governments developed similar models for filling their civil service vacancies.

In 1923, the Classification Act was passed. This law established the principle of equal pay for equal work, which the Civil Service Commission had been advocating for years.[12]

During the 1930s, merit systems expanded in state and local government. From the OPM: "According to a census taken in 1940 by the Civil Service Assembly of the United States and Canada, more than 850 cities had at least a portion of their employees under some type of merit system. Progress at the municipal level was greater than in county jurisdictions, where only 173 of the 3,053 counties had civil service systems."[13]

In 1939, the Hatch Act was passed. Its main provision was to prohibit federal employees from engaging in partisan political activity. The act also precluded federal employees from joining any political organization that advocated overthrowing the United States government.

In 1940, President Roosevelt signed the Ramspeck Act, which facilitated an unprecedented extension of the merit system. The act authorized the president to include almost any offices or positions in the executive branch within the competitive service, with relatively few exceptions.

World War II brought forth the Veterans' Preference Act of 1944, also known as the GI Bill. "This act redefined and consolidated into law certain benefits previously granted to veterans, either by law or regulation, and also added new benefits, some of which had the effect of amending the Civil Service Act."[14] Some of the key benefits were extra points, pass-over protection (i.e., veterans could not be "passed over" without approval), and the rule of three (i.e., selecting officials must choose from the top three candidates and they may not select a nonpreference eligible before selecting a higher-ranked preference eligible).

In 1948, Congress passed a law that banned discrimination against the hiring of physically handicapped persons for positions whose duties such persons could perform efficiently without endangering themselves or others.[15]

President Eisenhower established Schedule C in 1953. It excepted a new category of positions from the competitive service, as determined by the Civil Service Commission, because of their confidential or policy-determining character.

The following year, a new career-conditional appointment system was established by President Eisenhower, through an executive order. The system required that selectees, who were competitively appointed, serve a three-year conditional period before attaining full career status.

Under the Kennedy administration, Congress passed the Federal Salary Reform Act of 1962. Its purpose was to ensure that federal pay should be reasonably comparable to private sector pay for work of the same difficulty and responsibility. Congress also included a methodology for adjusting federal pay on an annual basis, which is commonly referred to as a cost-of-living adjustment (COLA).

In 1965, at the height of the Civil Rights movement, President Johnson assigned responsibility for equal employment opportunity in the federal service to the Civil Service Commission and declared that "it is the policy of the United States to provide equal opportunity in Federal employment for all qualified persons, to prohibit discrimination in employment because of race, creed, color, or national origin, and to promote the full realization of equal employment opportunity through a positive, continuing program in each executive department and agency."[16]

The Intergovernmental Personnel Act of 1970 "substantially increased the role of the Federal Government in advancing merit systems of employment at the State and local levels."[17]

Eight years later, Jimmy Carter signed the Civil Service Reform Act of 1978, which brought about many changes, including the development of a series of merit principles, the identification of prohibited personnel practices, the codification of labor relations into law, the establishment of the Federal Labor Relations Authority (FLRA) and the U.S. Merit Systems Protection Board (MSPB), and the creation of the Senior Executive Service (SES). The act also made it somewhat easier to remove federal employees for cause.

The Civil Service Reform Act also created the OPM, which replaced the Civil Service Commission. The OPM was given the

> authority to promulgate regulations for the merit system and to maintain programs to enable departments and agencies to establish, classify, and fill their jobs in the competitive service and to deal with their employees on all matters relating to employment throughout their careers—examination and

appointment, suitability and security, merit promotion, compensation, training, employee relations, awards and incentives, managerial and executive development, and employee benefits.[18]

However, the act did not fundamentally change the way that the government went about hiring prospective candidates.

President Carter also signed legislation allowing federal agencies to experiment with alternative work schedules (AWS), the idea of which was to make the government an employer of choice by giving its employees the opportunity to balance their work responsibilities and personal lives. President Reagan extended its use in 1982, and AWS became a permanent part of the civil service in 1985.

In 1980, the OPM established the Navy China Lake Project as a demonstration project, under the authority of the Civil Service Reform Act of 1978. This tested a more holistic approach to pay, performance appraisal, and position classification. The project involved pay banding, which used wider pay ranges in order to give supervisors more discretion in rewarding good performance.

Toward the end of President Carter's term, concerns arose regarding the diversity of the federal workforce. A court case was filed that alleged that the government's primary entry-level examination for administrative careers—the Professional and Administrative Careers Examination (PACE)—was discriminatory and had an adverse impact on the hiring of minorities for such positions in the federal government.[19] In response, the United States District Court for the District of Columbia approved a consent decree on November 19, 1981, that resolved a class-action suit known as *Angel G. Luevano, et al., v. Janice R. Lachance, Director, Office of Personnel Management, et al.* The plaintiffs alleged that PACE, which the Government had been using to hire many positions at the GS-5 and GS-7 levels, had an adverse impact on the employment of certain minorities for reasons that were not related to the jobs in question. The PACE examination was eventually abolished for all covered occupations.

It was first replaced by a program known as the Administrative Careers with America (ACWA) examination, which eventually made use of written questionnaires. After subsequent attempts to replace the PACE examination, written questionnaires came into general use to assess the experience and competencies of prospective candidates.

Of note is that the consent decree authorized a special hiring tool that allowed federal agencies to address the adverse impact on minorities in another way. Known as the Outstanding Scholar Program, it allowed federal agencies to hire college graduates who had a grade point average of 3.5 or better for certain positions at the grade GS-5 and GS-7 levels. This program is still in effect.

During the early years of the Reagan administration, there was a sense that the Civil Service Retirement System (CSRS) needed to change. Its design, which was based on an employee's "high-three" salary and length of service—the three consecutive years where an employee earned his or her highest salary—coupled with the employee's exclusion from Social Security, resulted in most employees staying with the government once they got a few years of service under their belts. In essence, Congress wanted to design a system that would provide for more portability.

As a result, Congress placed all new federal employees under Social Security and in 1987 it created a new Federal Employee Retirement System (FERS) that had three tiers: Social Security, a defined benefit retirement component, and a thrift savings plan. Current employees had the option of remaining under the CSRS or switching to the FERS. According to Tammy Flanagan of the National Institute of Transition Planning,

> The creators of FERS figured such compatibility would help agencies attract mid-career employees from private companies, and would enable federal employees to explore careers outside of government. When FERS employees leave federal service before retirement, they can take their Social Security benefits with them and roll over the funds in their Thrift Savings Plan accounts into private firms' 401(k) plans. They also can collect (defined benefit retirement component) as long as they complete a minimum of five years of federal service.[20]

This system remains in effect today.

In 1989, the Volcker Commission, which was created to address the "quiet crisis" in government (i.e., the decreasing attractiveness of government to prospective employees), made a series of recommendations to revitalize the federal public service. The commission focused on areas such as more flexible pay, improved training and development, an increase in the number of career civil servants at the senior level, and a series of reforms to enhance diversity at the federal level. This ultimately resulted in a 25 percent pay increase for executive schedule employees, which was then extended to employees in the SES.

The following year, the OPM initiated a study of white-collar civilian pay due to concerns that government pay was not competitive with private sector pay. The net result was the enactment of the Federal Employees Pay Comparability Act of 1990 (FEPCA). According to the OPM,

> FEPCA's most significant provisions included locality pay, which allows the Government to pay employees at the same grade level different rates of pay based on local labor market conditions, an annual pay adjustment process designed to close the overall disparity between Federal and non-Federal pay over a 9-year period, and discretionary authority to pay recruitment and relocation bonuses and retention allowances of up to 25 percent of basic pay.[21]

Unfortunately, locality pay has never been fully implemented due to complaints about the methodology used to compute the locality adjustments and the projected cost of closing the pay gap.

In 1993, Congress amended the Hatch Act to allow federal employees to take an active part in political campaigns for federal offices. Although federal employees were still prohibited from seeking office during partisan elections, most became free, while they were off duty, to work on the campaigns of the candidates of their choice.

President Bill Clinton came into office that same year and promised to "reinvent government." To accomplish this, he established the National Performance Review (NPR) under Vice President Al Gore. Its goals were "to make the entire federal government less expensive and more efficient, and to change the culture of our national bureaucracy away from complacency and entitlement toward initiative and empowerment."[22] The NPR issued almost four hundred major recommendations, including establishing more specific performance metrics, focusing on results, decentralizing many human resources management programs, and eliminating an enormous amount of paperwork, including the Federal Personnel Manual (FPM). NPR's efforts also led to the elimination of the federal government's universal application for employment, the SF-171.[23] Despite all its accomplishments, the reinventing government effort did not make any significant changes in the way that government supervisors were able to hire.

President George W. Bush's management agenda focused on five areas for improvement, one of which was improving the strategic management of human capital.[24] The guiding principles behind this approach were "that government should be: (1) citizen-centered, not bureaucracy centered; (2) results-oriented, not process oriented; and (3) market-based, actively promoting innovation through competition."[25]

Bush's management agenda's goal was to identify the skills required by employees to deliver the results that citizens desired and to make sure the employees have those skills, to reward outstanding performers, and to take action against poor performers.

One step forward was the establishment of the USAJOBS.gov Web site. This is the federal government's official recruitment site and the public's one-stop source for information on federal jobs and employment information. USAJOBS.gov provides government agencies with a recruitment mechanism that is easier to use, that is more consistent, and that reaches a greater percentage of the public.

USAJOBS.gov contains a good summary of relatively recent improvements in the federal government's processes:

> Many years ago, applicants who passed the civil service test were placed on standing registers of eligibles maintained by the Office of Personnel Management (OPM). In addition, applicants had to complete a standard Federal employment application form, the SF-171, to apply for all jobs.
>
> Today, the OPM no longer maintains registers of eligibles.
>
> ➤ Applicants can mail or fax their resume, or apply online using their resume in My USAJOBS. An optional application for Federal Employment, the OF-612, is also available for those who do not have a resume.

> ➤ Job seekers do not need a rating from OPM to enable them to apply for non-clerical vacancies.
> ➤ Only a few positions require a written test.
> ➤ The SF-171 is obsolete.[26]

With fifty state governments and more than eighty thousand local entities,[27] it is beyond this book's scope to review the history and evolution of recruitment at those levels. However, it is fair to say that many if not most state and local entities' approaches have evolved in a manner that roughly mirrors the federal government's. Some of these entities use written tests and compile civil service registers, and others simply rate and rank candidates based on their responses to questions. Still others use a combination of both approaches. However, almost every government agency now uses the Internet as a critical part of its recruitment strategy.

The laws can vary between levels, which is one reason why the systems do not completely mirror each other. For example, veterans' preference is applied differently across state, local, and federal governments. Many if not most state and local governments do not offer special recruitment authorities for college graduates who have 3.5 or higher indices (they were not affected by the consent decree discussed earlier). That having been said, I think it is fair to assert that the strengths and weaknesses of recruitment at the state and local levels are relatively similar to those at the federal level.

Outlook

Despite its evolution, government recruiting continues to be a complex, bureaucratic, and time-consuming process that tends to frustrate everyone involved and makes it seem as though the government is trying to prevent people from entering the system. Although some progress has been made at certain levels of government, I think that most people would agree that more progress needs to be made.

In his article "General Federal Hiring Practices," Eric Yoder provides a good description of the complexity of the process:

> While the government offers more job opportunities than most employers, its hiring practices are much stricter. In

order to comply with laws stating that hiring must be strict-
ly merit-based, the government's hiring process is a very
formal one. There's some debate as to whether that process
is more difficult for job-seekers than the more ad hoc procedures that a private sector company might use. But
there's no dispute that the government's process is a different one. "One of the differences is that the process is probably more regulated and regimented on the federal side
than it is on the private sector side. Much like small compa-
nies, you may not necessarily apply to the headquarters—
you actually apply to the plant that may be hiring," says
Ellen Tunstall, associate director for employment services at
the Office of Personnel Management (OPM), the government's central human resources agency. The government's
hiring process is much more decentralized than it was even
a decade ago. Much of the actual candidate evaluation takes
place at the individual agency that has the vacancy, not at
OPM. Listings of vacancies are available through centralized
sources, although understanding them is a skill in itself. "The
job announcements for federal agencies are very difficult to
understand for private industry people," says Kathryn
Troutman of The Resume Place, a speaker and author of
books on preparing resumes and job-seeking in the federal
government. "Also, the job titles are not the same as the job
titles in private industry. Another thing that's very hard for
many people is that each agency requires a different application format."[28]

I believe Yoder provides a fair description of the problem. From the perspective of a former personnel officer and a line manager and senior executive, the process always seemed slow and cumbersome.

When I was in personnel, we often had to deal with a wide variety of
rules and regulations that were difficult to both comprehend and implement. We had to handle a multitude of paperwork both to make our decisions and to justify our actions, and we frequently had to interact with outside sources (most notably the Civil Service Commission and then the OPM)
that were often overwhelmed, which made them slow to respond. By the

same token, internal customers wanting to know why we weren't filling their vacancies as quickly as they would like were constantly besieging us.

Of course, once I went into line management, I felt that same frustration. Although I understood what the personnel folks were going through, I too was not happy with their pace. Everything moved at a glacial speed, which was more a function of the system than of the employees. That's not to say that some of the personnel offices that I dealt with couldn't have been managed better; they most certainly could have. However, the common thread that they all had to deal with was an unwieldy system of complex rules and regulations.

Since I've retired, I've helped a number of people get jobs with the government.[29] Watching applicants try and weave their way through a maze of job announcements at various levels of government, I've been struck by how confusing, time-consuming, and frustrating they have found the process to be. In fact, roughly a third of the people I've worked with eventually gave up, not even bothering to go further. If you extrapolate their experiences to the pool of people who have an interest in working for the government but decide not to follow through, it is clear that the process alone screens out far too many potential candidates—and keep in mind that most candidates don't have access to someone like me who knows the system so well.

The OPM agrees that more work needs to be done. According to Angela Bailey, the OPM's Deputy Associate Director for Talent and Capacity Policy, "We are well aware the Federal hiring system has evolved over many years into a cumbersome process and hiring takes far too long. That is why we have expanded our efforts by partnering with several agency Chief Human Capital Officers to launch a new, holistic, and systemic view of the hiring process."[30]

As of this writing, the OPM plans to focus on the following:

> five interrelated components—workforce planning, recruitment, hiring, suitability and security, and orientation—that work in concert to create an efficient and effective hiring process . . . they will issue a Government-wide standard for the hiring process, along with a "how to" guide that includes successful practices, templates, and scripts for communicating with applicants.

As a subset of this initiative, the OPM is also streamlining job announcements and creating templates agencies may use when advertising for entry-level positions. "We have replaced the legalese and pages of extraneous information that were not necessary to announce a job," said Bailey. "It also advertises upfront two of the most important issues of concern to new professionals—pay and benefits."[31]

Regardless of the improvements that the OPM makes, I strongly suspect that every government organization, whether at the federal, state, or local level, will still have many challenges to recruiting top-notch candidates.

Look at Your Own Processes

While it is easy to blame the government's systems for your recruitment problems, sometimes you may find that the biggest problems lie at your own doorstep. Before you conclude that there is nothing more you can do to improve the way you go about recruiting, try and conduct a detailed analysis of your internal processes. You may find that there are a number of steps you can take to speed up the procedure.

To illustrate, most government recruitment processes go something like this: A vacancy occurs and the organization that has the vacancy submits a request to fill that vacancy (either electronically or by paper) to some sort of an internal budget or position management committee that decides whether or not that position should be filled. It may take that committee a week or two to decide whether it makes sense to fill the position, and sometimes may send the request back to the requesting official asking for further information, after which the process begins again.

Once approval is granted, the request goes next to position classification, which determines the title, series, and grade of the position. This may take anywhere from a day to a week or longer, depending upon whether the position description has been properly written, whether the form has been correctly filled out, and other criteria. Once that is accomplished, the request then goes to the recruitment section, which usually issues a vacancy announcement. The announcement may stay open for one, two, or three weeks or longer, depending on the organization's internal policy and its union contract, if any. The applicant may also have to wait a week or so after the announcement has closed to submit the requisite paperwork. This is also determined by internal policy or the union contract.

From this point, human resources management (HRM) has to rate and rank the internal candidates and will either rate the external candidates as well (assuming the organization is recruiting from the outside) or wait for an outside source, such as the OPM or a delegated examining unit (DEU), to prepare a certificate of external candidates. From there, applicants are interviewed, background checks are done, and, maybe, selections are made.

As you can see, this is a pretty cumbersome and time-consuming process for everyone concerned. The question is, does it need to be so difficult, or can some of the steps be bypassed? Let's examine the process in more detail to find out.

First of all, I would strongly encourage any government organization that does not have an electronic recruitment request and processing system to convert to such an approach as quickly as possible. After all, such a system would ensure that (1) the request moves instantly from one part of the organization to the next, (2) the organization can electronically track each step of the process and identify gaps, and (3) safeguards are built in so that if there are errors in the preparation of the document (e.g., the position number is not included in the request to fill the vacancy), the computer system will notify the requestor of the missing information.

Second, establish internal rules that allow organizations to bypass the budget/position management committee (e.g., when the requesting office is below ceiling and it is seeking to fill a multiencumbered position) or the position classification section under certain circumstances (e.g., if the job has been classified within the last year or two and the duties haven't changed). Of course, these entities should receive some form of electronic notice of the intent to bypass them so they know what is going on and are kept in the loop, and so that there is a formal record of all actions.

As another example, every vacancy does not have to be announced each time that it occurs. A better approach would be to use open continuous announcements, which let applicants apply for actual or prospective vacancies throughout the year. This way, when a vacancy occurs, a roster of candidates is already available, which saves management up to a month or longer in the overall process.

The above examples are simply illustrations of ways in which a government organization can speed up the recruitment process. Although they may or may not apply in every circumstance, this type of thinking is needed in order to make the process more government and applicant friendly.

While some degree of bureaucracy will always exist in government, the key is to understand the system that is in place, streamline it whenever possible, and use it to your best advantage. Moreover, you should begin to develop and implement a series of tried-and-true strategies that will best position your organization to take advantage of the talent that is available. The remainder of Section 1 will share these strategies with you.

CHAPTER

2

DEVELOPING
YOUR STRATEGY

IN MY EXPERIENCE, government managers typically recruit the old-fashioned way: They wait for a vacancy to develop and then submit a request to fill the position to the human resources management (HRM) activity that services them. The vacant position is then classified, a vacancy announcement is issued, interested applicants apply, applicants are rated and ranked, interviews are conducted, and a selection is finally made. All in all, several months usually transpire before the new employee reports for duty.

One of the problems with this approach is that it is reactive. Management literally waits for employees to leave and then reacts as events unfold. From HRM's point of view, it is merely following the system that is in place and doing what has been done for decades. However, from the line manager's point of view, a job remains unfilled while she is trying to keep up with what seems like an ever-increasing workload.

On the other hand, from a budget perspective, this waiting is not necessarily a bad thing; for every week that a position goes unfilled, the organization does not have to pay anyone to do that work. In a sense, the organization "makes money" whenever positions are unfilled because government organizations generally receive their payroll budget based on the number of projected full-time equivalent (FTE) employees[1] multiplied by the projected

19

average salary plus benefits per employee. Thus, if an activity spends an average of $52,000 per employee, and a position is vacant for four weeks, it will make $4,000 by not having to pay $1,000 per week for four weeks.

That is the math and you need to be aware of it—you should use it to help you manage your organization. However, do not let the budget drive you. After all, the driving force should be your organization's desire for excellent performance.

Let me give you an example. I once took over an organization where the budget officer was an overly dominant figure, and his actions often stifled everyone else. He would continually assert that the organization did not have much financial flexibility, and because he was the office expert on this subject, everyone would defer to him. The net result was that he kept the organization's money close to the vest, meaning that positions were not filled as quickly as they should have been, overtime was delayed, and supplies were not purchased as fast as possible.

The first time I met with this budget officer, I asked him how much excess funds we had in our budget (i.e., how much did we have to spend after we met our basic operating expenses, such as payroll, supplies, travel, and all else). He replied, "About $50,000." I responded that we probably had hundreds of thousands of dollars because, at our historical turnover rate of about nine percent, we were likely to lose about 40 people throughout the year. Moreover, because at that time we could expect lengthy delays from the time the jobs were vacated until they were filled again, we were going to "make money" every time someone left.[2] The officer did the math and reluctantly agreed that I was right.

In essence, because we had more money in the budget than the budget officer was telling us, we could plan on hiring more employees than we first thought and we could hire them earlier in the year—that is exactly what we did.

You might be asking yourself what this somewhat esoteric budget discussion has to do with hiring government employees. After all, isn't that the problem of the budget gurus and upper management? The answer is that if you leave the budget to other people who are not sensitive to its impact on operations, you run the risk of becoming a slave to the budget. The more you understand the budget process and use it hand in hand with sound recruitment strategies, the more resources you will have at your disposal and the better you will be able to perform. That is why I strongly advocate a concept I refer to as "anticipatory recruitment," wherein you do not always wait to hire until key positions become vacant.

Anticipatory Recruitment

Anticipatory recruitment simply means filling key positions, especially multi-encumbered positions,[3] *before* they become vacant. In essence, it is a form of succession planning wherein you carefully track such things as your annual turnover rate, your percentage of employees eligible to retire, and your potential performance-based or adverse actions and use this information to calculate your projected losses for the year. With this information in hand, coupled with solid workload projections, you can then determine the best time to bring on a class(es) of new employees—which sometimes means filling positions earlier than you would have if you were taking the traditional approach.

If done well, you will be able to mitigate the loss of experienced employees because you will already have their replacements in the pipeline. You will also ensure that the organization is constantly renewing itself, so you will not be "behind the eight ball," as many government organizations often find themselves. Furthermore, you can time this hiring to a period(s) when you can best release some of your key journeymen to train the new staff. Last, you will be able to perform better because you will have more horsepower available when you need it, rather than constantly waiting for the resources to catch up to the demands of your customers.

I am sure that this sounds all well and good to you. However, I also suspect you are wondering that if you take this approach, won't you be losing money because positions will no longer be vacant for appreciable periods and in fact may be filled on a duplicate basis? The answer is that this approach has its cost. However, you can successfully work within your budget while taking this approach, which will enable you to better achieve your mission, not merely save money in the short term.

Of course, sometimes you may want to accumulate some money for other needs and that is fine if that is part of an overall strategy. Remember, anticipatory recruitment is simply one more tool in your toolbox. The key is to use the budget to your advantage and not let the budget become the over-riding factor in managing your organization.

Let's look at two different approaches to managing the budget in the context of a recruitment strategy. The first approach is the traditional way.

Traditional Approach

Government organization X has 40 experienced customer contact represen-tatives (CCRs) whose job it is to both answer phone calls and respond to walk-in questions from the public. On average, each CCR costs $52,000 per year in salary and benefits, meaning that the budget for this activity is $2,080,000 ($52,000 x 40 = $2,080,000). For the sake of argument, let's assume that the organization expects to lose 10 percent of the CCRs this fis-cal year, or one at the beginning of each quarter. Let's also assume that each CCR takes one year to become fully trained and be considered a journey-man. Finally, let's assume that the organization takes about two months to fill each position (from the time an employee leaves until the time her replacement reports for duty), which is probably optimistic.

If the organization fills each vacancy in the traditional manner (i.e., after each person vacates her position), the organization will generate a total of about $32,000 in saved salary ($1,000 x 8 weeks = $8,000 x 4 employees = $32,000).[4] The $32,000 could be rerouted to overtime, purchasing supplies, or other activities.

On the other hand, every three months or so, as a CCR leaves, you first will have to redirect one or more supervisors from their normal job(s) to rank internal candidates for the vacancy announcement,[5] review job applications, interview prospective applicants, make selections, acquire a desk and phone, and ensure that a training program is set up.

You will then have to take a journeyman out of direct labor to train the new trainee. Moreover, either that journeyman or another one will also have to continue to work with the other trainees who were brought on board ear-lier in the year. By the end of the year, you will have four trainees on the rolls, all of whom will be at different experience levels and all of whom require periodic training until they reach the journeyman level.

Meanwhile, if you look back on the fiscal year, you will see that you have gone from 40 to 36 experienced CCRs (plus added four trainees with varying degrees of inexperience[6]), have lost a total of 32 man-weeks of direct labor (the four periods of eight weeks when positions were vacant) plus all of the time required to train the new hires, and redirected the activities of various supervisors and journeymen away from your direct mission in order to support the hiring and training of the four new hires—who would have, on average, 5.5 months of experience per person.

Although you will have "made" more than $32,000 due to the four positions becoming vacant, you will have paid an unacceptably heavy price in the reduction of your total capacity and your ability to serve your customers.

Anticipatory Recruitment Approach

Let's assume the same organization projects losing four CCRs in the manner previously described, but the organization decides to fill those projected losses at one time, on an anticipatory basis rather than on a piecemeal basis. The challenge will be to hire them at a time when you can afford them because the budget will only support having an average of no more than 40 CCRs throughout the year.

The best way to look at this is to make an annual projection. If you expect to lose one person on October 1,[7] one on January 1, one on April 1, and one on July 1, you can expect to lose a total of 30 man-months of CCRs, or the equivalent of two and one-half FTE over the fiscal year.[8] This means that if you chose to, you could afford to hire 2.5 additional CCRs on October 1 and still average 40 FTE CCRs for the year and not exceed your budget (assuming your projections are accurate).

However, note that you will save $130,000 if you lose the 2.5 journeymen CCRs ($52,000 x 2.5 = $130,000). Because you will most likely replace them with trainees, the cost to replace them will be a lot lower. For the purpose of this discussion, I am estimating that the total annual cost of a trainee will be $35,000 per person, including benefits. This means that you would have enough money in the budget to hire 3.7 FTE on October 1 ($130,000 / $35,000 = 3.7 FTE).

Because the goal in this situation would be to hire all four people at one time and as quickly as possible, let's see how you could do this. You cannot hire the four trainees on October 1 because you would be short $10,000; the four trainees would cost $140,000 for the year (4 x $35,000 = $140,000).

Because each trainee costs roughly $1,346 per pay period,[9] four trainees would cost $5,384 per pay period. If you plan on hiring all four of them after two pay periods, which is roughly the beginning of November, you can afford all four of them for the entire fiscal year.

Let's compare the outcome of this scenario with the traditional approach. Management will have to go through only one round of hiring instead of four. It will have to train only one group of employees during one period of time instead of training four individual employees at different points in time. It will have replacements for the employees it will be losing already on the rolls before most of those employees leave, meaning that the new employees can learn from the more experienced ones.

If you were to look back at the end of the fiscal year under this scenario, you will see that you have still gone from 40 to 36 experienced CCRs (plus added four trainees). However, you would have had far more man-weeks of available resources during the fiscal year than under the other scenario, and you would have redirected much less of your supervisors' and journeymen's time away from your mission to support the hiring and training of the four new hires. Moreover, the four trainees would now have an average of 11 man-months of experience, as compared to the 5.5 man-months if you followed the traditional approach—so you would be much further ahead of the curve.

Although you would not have the excess money that you would have had under the traditional approach, you would be using the money as intended, have more easily withstood the loss of trained employees, and be in a much better position to serve your customers and have a successful fiscal year.

Targeting Your Pool

Meeting your equal employment opportunity (EEO) goals and obligations is important and you need to factor this into your action planning. It is both the right thing to do and it will also help keep you out of trouble with respect to EEO issues, complaints from special interest and oversight groups, and other hassles. However, what is even more important is to develop an overall *strategy* for finding the best possible candidates (while achieving your EEO objectives) to help you meet your mission. After all, if you don't know who you want or how you will get them, you are likely to wind up with an unanticipated assortment of new employees—some who will meet your needs and some who most likely will not.

The better approach is to carefully assess the available pool of candidates relative to the competition, and then decide who you are going to target. By this I mean deciding in advance which groups of individuals would be the best possible fit for your organization and then determining how likely they would be to come to work for you and stay for the foreseeable future. Once you answer these questions, you should then know who to target.

The Vacancy Announcement

Before we explore this approach in more detail, it is important to emphasize that, in most cases, whenever a government entity has a vacancy and is opening it up to external candidates, a public vacancy announcement is required. This generally means that each vacancy announcement will be posted on that organization's Web site and/or on a broader Web site that advertises multi-agency government jobs (e.g., www.USAJobs.gov, www.50statejobs.com/gov, or www.GovernmentJobs.com), and it may be distributed to other venues as well. The point here is that when a government job is open to the public, in general you cannot exclude anyone from applying for the job, so your recruitment strategy must factor this in.

That having been said, you should never simply announce every vacancy by rote. Once you have targeted your recruitment pool, you should also decide what authorities are available to you and take advantage of them accordingly. This may mean that sometimes you will not announce a vacancy, while other times you will issue multiple announcements. Let's take a look at a couple of examples.

Say you are a federal employer and have applications from certain veterans who are entitled to a veterans' recruitment appointment (VRA).[10] Many of these individuals are excellent candidates because they have a demonstrated record of performance, bring with them a strong work ethic, and are highly motivated. If you have one or more vacancies and feel that VRAs would be a good fit, you could simply interview or select them without going through the whole vacancy announcement process. This would save an enormous amount of time and energy because you wouldn't have to write and issue an announcement, respond to inquiries from interested candidates, rate and rank candidates, and all the other requirements for filling the position. Moreover, you would probably save at least a month or more in the time it takes to go through the vacancy announcement process, meaning you would have the selectees on board quicker than if you were to follow the normal process.

Another way that federal employers can hire applicants without issuing a vacancy announcement is by hiring certain people with disabilities. The 5 C.F.R. 213.3102(u) enables "people with Mental Retardation, Severe Physical Disabilities, or Psychiatric Disabilities (who) have documentation from a licensed medical professional (e.g., a physician or other medical professional certified by a state, the District of Columbia, or a U.S. territory to practice medicine); a licensed vocational rehabilitation specialist (i.e., state or private); or any Federal agency, state agency, or agency of the District of Columbia or a U.S. territory that issues or provides disability benefits"[11] to apply for noncompetitive appointment[12] with the federal government.

Other programs available to federal employers that provide recruitment flexibility include but are not limited to the Outstanding Scholar Program, Bilingual/Bicultural Program, the 30 Percent Disabled Veteran Program, Student Temporary Employment Program (STEP), and the Student Career Experience Program (SCEP).[13] These types of special hiring authorities have been deemed to be in the public interest and are therefore available to federal employers.

Agencies at the state and local levels often have similar authorities available, although they vary at each level. For example, Maine allows agencies to directly hire prospective candidates for certain advanced professional or highly specialized technical jobs that usually have a license or certification requirement. It also allows agencies to directly hire for positions involving unskilled and semiskilled labor, attendant, domestic, or custodial duties.[14] Regardless of the level of government at which you are hiring, always be aware of the special hiring authorities that are at your disposal and use them to your best advantage.

Announcing a job at several different grade levels is another way to build in additional flexibility (e.g., announcing a Personnel Management Specialist GS-201-05/07/09/11, meaning you will accept applications at each grade level). By taking this approach, you are establishing a different civil service certificate of eligible candidates at each grade level, even though you may wind up filling only one job at one grade level.

The advantage of this approach is that you will have a wider range of candidates with broader experience to choose from because you will have four different certificates at four separate grade levels. In addition, you may have someone you are interested in who is not selectable at one grade level (perhaps because she is blocked by a veteran or is not among the top three candidates on the list[15]) who is selectable at either a higher or lower grade.

The downside is that this approach requires a lot more work. Instead of issuing one announcement, you are issuing four. You will now have to rate and rank far more candidates and you will have to interview a greater number than had you simply issued one announcement at one grade level. The key here is to be aware of all of your available options and then use them wisely.

Assuming you issue a vacancy announcement, it should include the title, series, grade(s), and/or pay of the job; the name of the employing agency; the location of the position; and the opening and closing dates. It should also include the duties and qualifications of the job, a section on how to apply, information on pay and benefits, and other pertinent information. The announcement is usually then posted on the Internet and may be distributed by mail to certain organizations, such as the Department of Labor.

That being said, as long as you follow the rules with respect to where you are required to advertise a government job, there is nothing to prevent you from distributing your announcement to additional targeted locations, organizations, schools, or groups. This would include sending copies of your announcements to whomever you think might be interested and would give you the best bang for the buck. Your strategy could also include participating in local job fairs or establishing booths at local colleges to try and attract future graduates.

I would like to include a note of caution before I proceed. Although soliciting a large number of applications for your vacancies can be a good thing, it also can have its downside. For example, if you take a "scattergun" approach to recruitment, resulting in an overwhelming number of applications, you may find that other weaker candidates will block some of the candidates you really want to hire. This may be because you receive a large number of applications from veterans; people who are good at writing job applications; individuals who worked for the government for many years and did not get ahead, but who on paper may wind up being ranked higher than less experienced but more talented individuals; or a combination of these groups.

The point here is that you "get what you design for." So if you design a carefully targeted recruitment program, odds are that you will get what you want. If you do not, who knows who you will end up getting.

Deciding Who to Target

The first thing you need to decide are the key competencies for the job or jobs you will be filling. Once you know these, you should determine what would be the pool(s) of candidates with the greatest potential for success. For example, if you are looking to fill a number of jobs where a college degree would be highly desirable (e.g., financial analysts, technical writers, or HRM specialists), the traditional approach would be to try and hire recent college graduates who are outstanding scholars. The rationale behind this approach would be that they are probably the best and the brightest of the available candidates, and certain levels of government (especially at the federal level) are authorized to hire these individuals on the spot without going through the normal civil service process.

The problem is that this approach doesn't work in every part of the country, especially in high-cost areas. According to one newspaper article, "This is the 'new economy,' where most of the rules are different. The days of staying at a company long enough to get that prized gold Rolex are gone, gone, gone. . . . Workers today are like the proverbial rolling stone. The National Research Bureau recently reported that the average employee changes jobs every three or four years."[16]

In a high-cost area, where there are many opportunities for recent graduates and where government salaries are not overly competitive, I suspect you will find that even if you can hire outstanding scholars, you will probably lose many of them pretty quickly. That has been my experience and the experience of many of my colleagues. Given the inclination of recent graduates to change jobs often, this is not very surprising.

On the other hand, for my peers who recruit in lower-cost areas, government jobs can be attractive to outstanding scholars because the salaries are competitive and the jobs are interesting and offer much more security than the private sector. In this case, recruiting outstanding scholars makes perfect business sense and is the right thing to do.

When I was Director of VA's Los Angeles Regional Office, we struggled to retain new employees, in part because of the cost of living in the area and in part because so many younger employees tended to change jobs very frequently. I therefore took a different approach and targeted older segments of the population, particularly candidates over age 35. My rationale was that many of these people had probably been kicking around for a while, now had broader family obligations, and were looking for more stability so they would be less likely to leave. Moreover, most of them were college graduates and were quite bright, were savvy about the real world, and brought a strong work ethic to the table. In my particular situation (i.e., managing a large government office in Los Angeles), targeting this population group made perfect sense.

While I was writing his book, the economy took a major turn for the worse and, consequently, government jobs, with their relatively high degree of security, are now more attractive to recent college graduates even in high-cost areas. Changing economic situations are both normal and cyclical, even though this one is one of the worst we have seen. This is normal and to be expected and should be factored into your recruitment planning. The point here is that your hiring strategy should be flexible and allowed to evolve as your situation changes. That being said, you will also need to ask yourself how long you will be able to retain these employees once the economy turns around and jobs in the private sector are again plentiful.

Let's take a look at another strategy that was situational in nature that worked well. An organization that I am familiar with was looking to hire people to evaluate medical claims for government benefits. These jobs were quasi-legal in nature and required a high degree of reading, writing, and analytical skill. Typically, an internal pool of claims processors filled these positions, with the best technicians being promoted into these jobs. Nearly every office in the nation took this approach.

This particular organization decided to take a different approach. Recognizing that it was working in a low-cost area and could attract a large pool of candidates, it decided to target attorneys as its recruitment pool. Attorneys were "a dime a dozen" in this area of the country and many attorneys were more than happy to go to work for the government.

The rationale for hiring attorneys was that they could bring a different skills mix to the table than could internal claims processors, and they therefore would make more accurate decisions that were better written and more easily defensible. This, in fact, proved to be the case for this particular office, and its recruitment strategy played a major role in their success.

Unfortunately, this approach was not replicated across the country because each area had a different set of circumstances. Some offices' recruitment efforts decided to target nurses because nurses were already familiar with medical terminology and, therefore, would require far less training. Other offices actually recruited from local government agencies whose mission also involved evaluating claims for medical benefits. Obviously, this approach might have helped that office but it did not help the government as a whole. The organizations with the most successful recruitment efforts were those that crafted a comprehensive strategy geared to their particular situation and needs.

Back in the 1970s, as the Vietnam War was winding down, the U.S. Department of Veterans Affairs (then known as the Veterans' Administration) was facing an onslaught of veterans returning from the war who would need assistance with health care, benefits, and finding jobs. To address this workload, both the administration and Congress knew that they would need more employees.

The VA turned to the perfect pool of candidates—America's veterans. It hired them through a variety of programs and authorities (such as the disabled veteran program), which proved to be a great boon for the VA. These individuals were dedicated and driven to succeed, and they brought a great work ethic. Moreover, because they served in the military, they were much more likely to understand the needs of returning veterans. Many of them rose to the highest ranks of the VA, becoming secretaries, undersecretaries, program directors, senior executives, division or service chiefs, physicians, nurses, or scientists, and they continue to make major contributions today.

Nearly all agencies at every level of government followed the VA's lead and hired veterans for many of the same reasons. They too experienced a great deal of success with this group of individuals. To put things in perspective, one study found the following:

The federal Government remains the Nation's leading employer of veterans. Some 462,744 veterans—over one out of every four federal workers—are employed today in agencies across the country and around the world. FY 2007 hiring data from agency members of the President's Management Council, which represent 97.6% of all Federal workers, show these agencies employ 457,645 veterans. Independent agencies reported approximately 5,100 of their employees are veterans. Overall, total veteran new hires in the federal government have increased from 50,108 in FY 2006 to 52,452 in FY 2007.

In comparison to the private sector, the federal government hires three times the number of veterans, seven times the number of disabled veterans, and 10 times the number of severely injured veterans.[17]

With the wars in Iraq and Afghanistan, eventually we can expect to see another major outflow of veterans into the civilian population. Government agencies would be wise to target this group of individuals for recruitment again.

Let's look at another situation. An office that I knew had tremendous difficulty in recruiting and retaining clerks. Pay in that particular area of the country was too low to attract many people and the nature of the job itself (filing claims folders all day) resulted in the few people who it could hire leaving after a relatively short period of time. Management felt that it was dealing with a vicious cycle of recruitment, training, and loss, and they finally decided to take a different approach. They targeted the hearing impaired, knowing that many of these individuals had a difficult time finding a job and would therefore be more likely to stay, as compared to the typical candidates they were finding from the general recruitment population.

They hired about 20 people who were hearing impaired, along with a full-time translator, and quickly found that this made a significant difference. These individuals were grateful to have a government job, had a relatively good work ethic, and did not look to find other jobs.

On the other hand, the experience was problematic because supervisors had a hard time communicating with these employees when the translator was not available. To make matters even more difficult, the office quickly found out that people who are hearing impaired process information differently from the way that non-hearing-impaired people do, so communication became a real challenge.

Eventually, several of the supervisors took classes on how to use sign language, and this made the situation somewhat easier to deal with.

Although hiring the hearing impaired was not a perfect solution to this office's problems with respect to the recruitment and retention of clerks, it was a step forward and greatly reduced the turnover rate in this particular occupation. On balance, targeting this particular class proved to be a good thing, and 20 years later many members of that original class continue to work for their government employer in the same capacity.[18]

I recall a different government organization that also had a unique challenge. Every year, for a fixed period of time, it had to review financial records of a certain segment of clients in order to ensure that the clients were receiving the benefits they were entitled to. This required the organization's management to hire a temporary group of employees each year to address this situation, which was a complicated challenge. After all, they had to hire them, train them, and then let them go once the project was completed—and then start all over again.

Initially, this office hired high school students to take on the task. There were plenty of them in the labor pool, they were easy to hire, and they were relatively quick learners. However, management finally concluded that high school students did not, by and large, possess the maturity that they were looking for and they decided to hire local college students instead. This proved to be the solution, as the college students were certainly more mature than the high school students and they were eager to impress their employer, knowing that the job might lead to a full-time position with the government. Eventually, this is exactly what happened, with some of the students even dropping out of school to work for this organization full time while others went to work for it after graduating college.

The point of these examples is that government recruitment is often a self-fulfilling prophecy. Although there is no doubt that government recruiters certainly have their challenges, particularly in high-cost areas, they do not have to sit idly by and be victims either. If you carefully plot out a recruitment strategy, based on a keen understanding of the jobs you are recruiting for, as well as the potential pools of candidates that are available in the job market, you may find that recruitment is not as difficult as you had originally thought.

Expect the Unexpected

Before we go forward, I want to add a word of caution: Because you are working for the government, you need to recognize that there are always a wide variety of forces at play and, accordingly, they sometimes can impact your staffing efforts. For example, if your organization or another government agency at the same level is consolidating or cutting back, a career transition assistance plan will probably cover the affected employees. In the event that you have a vacancy, you will probably be required to select these displaced employees ahead of most other candidates, assuming they are qualified for the position.

Although this can be frustrating and can prevent you from selecting the people you would prefer, you need to recognize that there may come a time when you will be displaced, so from that perspective having such a program is comforting. The best thing you can do is keep informed about any reductions-in-forces (RIFs) that are going on in your area, so that you can adjust your strategy as appropriate. For instance, if you hear that an RIF is about to occur, and the affected employees are less than desirable, it may be a good idea to try and fill your vacancies, or anticipated vacancies, before the RIF is completed. On the other hand, displaced employees can provide you with a ready source of dedicated and experienced talent. So weigh your approach carefully before crafting your strategy.

As another example of the unexpected, sometimes you may be in the middle of recruiting and get hit with a local, agency-wide, or government-wide hiring freeze that stops your recruiting efforts in their tracks. That is one of the most difficult situations that you may have to deal with as a government manager. I recall one time when I was running a government organization and we had just interviewed well over 20 people in order to fill 10 vacancies. We made our selections and were about to notify the candidates when our headquarters instructed us to stop our recruitment efforts due to a national hiring freeze. Imagine how annoyed we were, given that we had already put a tremendous amount of work into announcing the jobs, screening the candidates, and interviewing so many people.

This was a situation that was tough to foresee because it was imposed by a new acting undersecretary, right after the previous one had been summarily dismissed. No one saw it coming, but this happens sometimes in government.

However, on other occasions, you certainly can see the freeze coming. For example, when I was working for the Department of Defense in the 1970s, I knew that my job was in jeopardy due to local cutbacks, so I tried to find a job with another agency. The U.S. General Services Administration took an interest in me and decided to interview me as quickly as possible, which meant that Saturday. Their rationale was that a government-wide hiring freeze was to be imposed the following Monday, so they interviewed and hired me before the freeze occurred.

Looking ahead, as of this writing, many state and local governments are currently in hiring freezes because the economic downturn has adversely affected their tax revenues. Conversely, at the federal level, we will likely see a significant amount of hiring because President Obama has vowed to create many jobs in the public sector in order to stimulate the economy. As always, the ground is constantly shifting in government.

Where and How to Advertise

The best way to develop your advertising plan is to make sure that it focuses on the group(s) of potential candidates who you are targeting. For example, if you are going after Hispanic candidates, make sure that you are advertising in the local Spanish-speaking media. Also, make sure that you are communicating with your local Hispanic employment program coordinator, if you have one, and leveraging her expertise to access the candidates from the Hispanic community. Last, make sure that your job announcements are written in both English and Spanish.

If you are targeting older workers (they are often an excellent but untapped source of candidates for government jobs due to their experience, work ethic, and availability), make sure that you are placing advertisements in publications that cater to older workers, such as the American Association of Retired Person's magazine (now known simply as AARP). Recognize that this particular group of potential candidates is probably not as computer literate as other groups, so do not rely exclusively on Web sites to get their attention. Finally, establish a relationship with community and government groups that assist older people because these groups will be more in tune with older workers' interests and issues and they will be able to steer you in the right direction.

Should you decide to target veterans, consider advertising in some of the publications that cater to the military, such as *Stars and Stripes Magazine*. Also look at placing ads in some of the magazines that are published by veterans' service organizations, such as the *American Legion, Disabled American Veterans,* and the *Military Order of the Purple Heart.* Naturally, you also want to coordinate your efforts with the U.S. Department of Veterans Affairs, especially its Vocational Rehabilitation Division, as well as any state and local government entities that help serve veterans.

The point here is that you want to coordinate your recruitment efforts so that you are attracting candidates who will be good fits for your organization. If you do this well, you will create a self-fulfilling prophecy: You will hire the people who have the knowledge, skills, and abilities that your organization needs for it to be successful.

If you don't target your efforts but simply take the scattergun approach (i.e., try to attract as many people as possible without a particular strategy in mind), you will do what many if not most government recruiters do, which is attract a reasonable pool of candidates, some of whom will be good and some of whom will not be. This will eventually force you to terminate the worst of your selections during probation,[19] after which, if you don't develop a comprehensive strategy, the cycle will continue.

Getting Out into the Market

An important part of any good recruitment strategy is to get out into the market, find good candidates, and convince them to apply to your organization. This typically entails sending representatives of your agency out to job fairs, college activities, and other community events in order to solicit applications from the best possible candidates.

This is a great opportunity to shape the perceptions of prospective applicants regarding your organization. Accordingly, you want to make sure that you send the best possible representative to these events because you need someone there who can demonstrate to people why they should come work for you. Unfortunately, far too often, the government sends grizzled and relatively cynical HRM specialists to college fairs in order to try and persuade college students that the government is right for them. The problem is, these HRM individuals often convey a negative message to students about the benefits of government service, and students immediately pick up on it and conclude that they do not want to work with individuals who display such an unpleasant attitude. Moreover, because these HRM specialists often come from a different generation, they are unable to relate to students as easily as someone who is closer in age to the students. Last, because these representatives are HRM experts but are not experts in the field(s) that they are recruiting for, on many occasions they cannot satisfactorily answer the students' questions.

A better approach would be to send representatives who are experts in the area(s) you are recruiting for and who are closer in age and have similar interests to the individuals you are looking to attract. These recruiters should have the ability to establish an immediate rapport with prospective candidates and be able to answer their technical questions, speak their language, and size them up. Recruiters who can do all that will clearly be your best salespeople and will attract the highest number of strong candidates.

Let's look at a few other examples. If you are looking for nurses, would you send male recruiters who do not know anything about the medical field to nursing schools? I don't think so. Although there are obviously some males who go into nursing, it is still dominated by women, so it seems logical that experienced female nurses who are outgoing and personable would, for the most part, be the best choice to serve as recruiters.

If you are looking for engineers or scientists, you would want to have accomplished people in that field represent you. They would command the respect and admiration of future professionals in a way that an HRM specialist could not.

That's not to say that HRM specialists should not be involved in the recruitment process because I believe they most certainly should. They should be present in a support capacity to answer questions about the recruitment process, promotional opportunities, and benefits. In my experience, a combination of a charismatic, people-friendly technical expert along with a savvy HRM specialist is the best way to conduct on-site recruitment and attract the best candidates.

Making Your Organization More Desirable

An important component of recruitment is making your organization more desirable to outside candidates. People form their impressions about the government and your organization in particular from a number of different sources, so it only stands to reason that the more attractive you can make your organization to prospective candidates, the more likely they are to apply for jobs with you. If you go out to a job fair and merely sit in a blank booth with no material outlining why someone should go to work for you, odds arc that most people will not want to join your team. Why not put together some first-class displays that highlight your mission, explain what you are all about, and show what you have to offer? That approach will certainly get the people's attention.

In addition, you should develop one or more quality brochures or pamphlets that potential employees can read. This material should show your organization in the best possible light and make the case for why someone would want to join you. Use attractive pictures and professional language to (1) focus on the importance of your mission, (2) remind the reader that your agency provides a great opportunity to make a difference and it values people, and (3) emphasize the career opportunities that you have to offer and make your case as to why someone should come to work for you.

By all means, use the Internet as another opportunity to shape the outside world's view of your organization. Many government organizations now take this approach. For example, the United States Federal Aviation Administration's (FAA) Web site has a section entitled "Jobs and Careers" that displays the following information:

- ➤ Current FAA job openings
- ➤ Major occupations at FAA
- ➤ Executive opportunities
- ➤ International Civil Aviation Organization (ICAO) positions

➤   Student programs

➤   Veteran's employment program

➤   Application forms[20]

If you were to click on the link for "major occupations" at FAA, you would be able to view the following information:

> We operate the largest aviation system in the world. We are responsible for the safety and certification of aircraft and pilots, around-the-clock operation of our nation's air traffic control system, and for the regulation of U.S. commercial space transportation.
>
> We're looking for employees to help us maintain our place as the world leader in aviation. Your ambition can take you places at the FAA.[21]

If you click further, you can learn more about key jobs, such as air traffic controller, air transportation systems specialist, or aviation safety inspector. Further links will tell you how to apply for these jobs, which licenses and certificates may be required, and other useful information.

My only criticism of the FAA's Web site is that it does not contain any visuals that would convey a deeper sense of what it has to offer. If it included photographs of FAA employees in action or images of some of its more dynamic work sites, the Web site would be much more exciting and attractive to prospective candidates.

In contrast to the FAA's site is the state of Ohio's Hiring Management System Web site.[22] This site similarly contains job information, but it also includes a series of flashing pictures of smiling employees, accompanied by words such as "opportunity," "commitment," "public service," "balance," and "people." It also features a section on "Why choose a career in public service," which emphasizes the value and importance of working for the government. To me, this overall approach, which includes both important information but also makes an emotional pitch to Web site visitors, is the way to go.

Another way to sell your organization to prospective applicants is through the design of your physical plant. Potential employees visit government buildings all the time for a variety of reasons: to get a passport, to pick up tax forms, to file a claim for benefits. During these visits, they quickly form an impression of the agencies there, and if all they see is typical government-gray office space with nondescript walls, dark interiors, and shabbily dressed employees, do you think they will want to work for that organization at a later date? I think not.

In the book *Seeing Is Believing*, co-authored with Pamela Posey, we suggest that the reader do the following:

> Imagine an organization that is a work of art, one that uses all the effective management tools and also the tools of an artist to produce an environment that is designed to work great. Imagine a vision statement that is more than just a bunch of words, one that captures the mission, vision, and guiding principles of the organization with a compelling image on a single page. Imagine a physical plant that is bright, airy, and open, one that has the most effective work flow and a workspace that allows people to concentrate on their individual tasks and work together as a team. Imagine a workplace in which the walls, floors, and ceilings are decorated with a coordinated set of pictures, sculptures, banners, flags, and other displays that are all designed to link people directly to the organization's mission. Imagine that the employees are so proud of the workplace of which they are a part that they bring their families to see it. Imagine a workplace that is so visually coherent that it can instantly shape the impression or point of view of the outside world the minute the visitor enters. Visually, this would be a place that is special, a place that is filled with innovation and creativity.[23]

Such places do exist in government. For example, the VA's Central California Healthcare System's workspace celebrates its mission and honors its employees. According to its Director, Al Perry,

> Over a 5-year period we continuously upgraded our medical
> center interiors using visual management principles. We're
> told the art, photomontages, murals, life-size cutouts, monu-
> ments, flags, and displays have deeply affected both patients
> and staff. Patients derive a sense of welcome, belonging, and
> respect. They feel a clear sense of history, sacrifice, and mil-
> itary mission. Many staff have remarked how proud they are
> to walk under the large American flag and bold sign
> inscribed, "The Price of Freedom Is Visible Here."

Opposite are a few photographs that will give you some sense of the Central California Healthcare System's visual management program and how it will affect not only veterans and employees but also prospective employees.

Any government organization that takes such an approach will instantly create a positive first impression with visitors and potential employees. Why? Because visitors will see a workspace that is not typical of government. It is a workspace that is fresh, alive, and exciting and one that values its employees. In the long run, this type of environment will attract dedicated people.

Don't Forget the People Who Already Work for You

In our desire to refresh the organization by bringing on board new and talented people, it is easy to forget all of the employees who currently work for us. Keep in mind that these are the folks who have been getting the job done in many cases for years if not decades. These are the people who invariably train the new employees, show them the ropes, and help facilitate their careers. Naturally, over time, many of these experienced employees become resentful if they conclude that all the organization cares about are the new employees. After all, from their perspective, they wonder why they are constantly being asked to train people who will quickly surpass them, knowing that many of these same people are likely to leave the organization for bigger and better opportunities, leaving them to then train the next group of new employees.

The fact of the matter is that these experienced employees have a point. They are the ones who usually stay with the local organization for the long

Figure 2-1: As soon as anyone walks into this space, they can see that this is a welcoming environment that honors veterans.

Figure 2-2: Every inch of space is used to remind people why the VA exists.

Figure 2-3: At the same time, the good work of employees is constantly being celebrated.

term, and they need to be treated with respect and dignity and be given the opportunity to advance when appropriate.

That is not to say that every long-standing employee deserves a promotion because of their tenure with the organization; they do not. After all, we all know plenty of employees who have already reached the highest level at which they are capable of performing. In fact, one of the worst things you can do is promote someone just because he has worked for you for a long time. This sends a message that time on the job counts, not performance. You want to avoid this scenario at all costs.

That being said, there are plenty of employees, including people who have little or no college education, who can and should be promoted. These employees have the requisite experience, the institutional memory, the work ethic, and the desire to succeed and they should be given the opportunity to get ahead. They should be promoted for no other reason except that it is the right thing to do; it is the right thing for the organization and the right thing for the employees.

Throughout my career, I have seen employees who started out at the bottom of the pecking order—clerks and secretaries—successfully advance and become technicians, journeymen, supervisors, division chiefs, and even senior executives. They moved up because they were good employees, they worked hard, and they deserved to be promoted. Their promotions sent a powerful message to the rest of the workforce: that anyone could rise in the organization as long as they earned it.

Of course you probably have a fair number of employees in your organization who think they deserve promotions when in reality they don't. If that happens, management is most likely to blame, not the employees, because one of management's jobs is to be honest with the employees and let them know how they are doing and what they need to do to improve.

In my experience, the reason why so many long-term employees become frustrated with their career limitations is because no one in management has ever been honest with them. If employees understand their shortcomings and don't correct them, then they have no one to blame but themselves. On the other hand, if they think they are not getting promoted because management has something against them or does not believe in promoting from within, they are going to become angry or cynical and not "give it their all."

The bottom line is that whenever you are looking to fill vacancies, you should never forget the people who are currently working for you. When filling multiple positions, in most cases, an appropriate mix of internal selections coupled with outside hires is the way to go.

3

SCREENING AND INTERVIEWING THE CANDIDATES

Screening

Now that you have gone through the recruitment process and solicited a reasonable number of candidates, the next step is to screen the applicants. This means you must rate and then rank the candidates.

Rating

By *rating*, I mean having a staffing specialist evaluate the education, experience, and other job-related training of each applicant against the qualification standards for the position in question.

The Federal Jobs Network Web site states, "Qualification standards are intended to identify applicants who are likely to be able to perform successfully on the job, and to screen out those who are unlikely to do so."[1] To put it another way, qualification standards are used to determine who meets the minimum qualification requirements for a position and who does not.

For example, the Department of Defense, Defense Contract Audit Agency, was looking for an office automation assistant, GS-0326-05/06.[2] Listed below are the qualifications requirements for the job:

One (1) year of specialized experience equivalent in level of difficulty and responsibility to that of the next lower grade in the federal service or comparable in difficulty and responsibility to the equivalent grade level if outside the federal service which demonstrates the ability to perform the duties of the position.

For GS-05: Experience performing a variety of administrative support functions which includes the use of office automation software (word processing, spreadsheet and databases); retrieval, update and storage of electronic data; preparing, editing and final formatting of documents and reports; making travel arrangements; processing mail; files management and customer support/telephone coverage.

For GS-06: Includes the above, and experience providing a variety of support services to include updating and maintaining automated information systems, software updates, equipment configuration, user access support, and related functions.

In addition, applicants must be able to type 40 words per minute in order to qualify for this position.

Substitution of Education for Specialized Experience:

To be creditable, education must have been obtained in an accredited business, secretarial or technical school, junior college, college or university.

For GS-05: Four years of successfully completed education above the high school level in any field for which high school graduation, or the equivalent, is a prerequisite may be substituted to meet the specialized experience required. Equivalent combinations of successfully completed post-high school education and experience may be used to meet total experience requirements. Only education in excess of the first 60 semester hours (i.e., beyond the second year) is creditable.

For GS-06: Six (6) months of graduate education may be substituted to meet the specialized experience required when it is directly related to the work of the position being filled. Equivalent combinations of education and experience may be used to meet total experience requirements.3

All applicants for this position would be rated against the above standards to determine basic eligibility. The organization's staffing specialist who handles this position would rate internal candidates, and the same person or an outside organization, such as the Office of Personnel Management (OPM) or a delegate examining unit (DEU), depending upon the policy of that particular level of government, would rate external candidates.

Given the pay grades for positions at this level, it is not easy to find good candidates, particularly in high-cost areas. Therefore, staffing specialists should take a relatively liberal approach to rating candidates at the lower grades.There is no point using a strict constructionist approach to reviewing qualifications at this level. If you do, odds are you will screen out an unacceptable number of candidates. Unfortunately, I have seen this happen time and time again. It is infuriating if you are a manager trying to find good candidates for your vacancies.

That is not to say that you should disregard the qualification standards either. They are there for a reason, which is to ensure that only qualified candidates are considered for vacancies. Rating candidates is as much an art as it is a science because of the many gray areas in the rating process.

For the above vacancy of office automation specialist, the key phrase is that an applicant's experience must "demonstrate the ability to perform the duties of the position."4 Some staffing specialists might interpret this to mean that a candidate's resume would have to show that she performed duties that were similar to those described in the vacancy announcement and position description. I would not. To me, at this level, what the qualification standard is really looking for is experience that would be a good predictor that the applicant could do the job. High school students routinely perform many of the tasks that are shown as creditable experience (e.g., the use of office automation software or formatting documents). As long as applicants state that they have performed these or analogous tasks within the context of their previous experience (without even substituting their education for experience), I would probably qualify them for this position.

Ultimately, staffing specialists who use common sense to rate applicants will ensure that the process works as smoothly and effectively as possible.

Let's look at a government job at a higher level. Denver, Colorado, was recently looking for an associate information technology systems administrator to work at the Denver Airport. Listed below were the qualifications for the job:

> Operating knowledge of UNIX/LINUX, Microsoft operating systems, specifically UNIX/LINUX, Windows XP, Windows Server 2003, VERITAS Cluster Server, Oracle Database and Web based application delivery. Some experience with project management principles and ITIL models; IT-specific service desk applications and processes; Cisco telecommunication switchers and Ethernet fabrics, specifically Cisco devices; Wide Area Network communication experience is expected but not required.

> BA/BS in an Information Technology major or other related technical discipline and three (3) years professional-level experience encompassing domain management, user management, relational database support, server and workstation management and peripheral support, networking and application-level support.

> Equivalency: Additional years of experience relevant to this position may be substituted for each year of education required: required one year of (Installation & Configuration).

> Ideal candidate will have working knowledge and experience with: LINUX, Veritas Cluster Servicer, Veritas Volume and BASH Scripting Manger.[5]

For a job at this level, staffing specialists should take a more conservative approach to rating candidates. After all, this is a job that requires a high degree of skill and the selectee must be able to be off and running on day one. To put this into perspective, the position description states that the incumbent "performs full-spectrum professional level work creating, analyzing, implementing, maintaining, supporting and documenting complex, integrated, site wide computer-based systems."[6]

In this case, the agency cannot afford to bring on someone who has a general understanding of the job and can grow into it over time. That could potentially be disastrous at the fourth busiest airport in the nation and the eleventh busiest in the world. In this particular case, and for most upper-level, skilled positions, common sense dictates that staffing specialists take a more conservative approach toward rating candidates.

The question then is, how do you know when to be conservative and when to be liberal? Beyond the general guidelines I have already provided, I suggest that you always keep the following rule of thumb in mind: Rate every applicant using the same philosophical approach. In other words, if (1) every applicant is treated the same way, meaning that the qualifications standards are applied equally to all; (2) you make decisions that are consistent with the letter and the spirit of the standards; and (3) you apply them with an equal dose of common sense, you will facilitate an effective and efficient rating process.

On occasion, selective factors are used as part of the rating process. According to the OPM standards, these are specific qualifications that

> are absolutely required because a person cannot perform successfully in the position without such qualifications. These can include requirements for specific KSA's [Knowledge, Skill, and Ability] or federal or state requirements for licensure or certification. . . . A selective factor becomes part of the minimum requirements for a position, and applicants who do not meet it are ineligible for further consideration.[7]

A good example of a selective factor would be an occupation that requires fluency in Spanish. Again, according to the OPM standards,

> Selective factors cannot (1) be so narrow that they preclude from consideration applicants who could perform the duties of the position, (2) require KSA's that could be learned readily during the normal period of orientation to the position, (3) be so specific as to exclude from consideration applicants without prior Federal experience, or (4) be so restrictive that

they run counter to the goal of placing applicants from priority placement lists established to assist in the placement of employees affected by reductions in force.[8]

If you plan to use selective factors, they should be listed on the vacancy announcement so that all candidates are aware of the requirements.

You can also use quality ranking factors as another way to narrow the field. Quality ranking factors are not as restrictive as selective factors, and the OPM defines them as follows:

> Quality ranking factors are KSAs/competencies that significantly enhance performance in a position, but, unlike selective factors, are not essential for satisfactory performance. Agencies should rank applicants with higher proficiency levels on a quality ranking factor above those with lower proficiency levels. Agencies may not rate qualified candidates ineligible solely for failure to possess a quality ranking factor. With quality ranking factors, the focus is on the level of proficiency the candidate brings to the job.[9]

The KSAs used as quality ranking factors may have been obtained through experience or education. Accordingly, related educational courses can demonstrate the possession of quality ranking factors. This would be particularly true at entry-grade levels where many applicants may not possess experience that demonstrates the applicable KSAs. For example, a financial analyst job may have duties such as analyzing the financial status of components in an agency. While no particular courses are required for basic eligibility as a financial analyst, for applicants who meet the education qualification requirements, courses on finance, business, or economics should be expected in order to enhance performance in the position.

The state of Georgia frequently uses a similar approach. The minimum qualifications for each vacancy (in terms of work experience and education or training) are usually identified on each announcement. Applicants must have these qualifications in order to be considered for the job. However, you often see preferred qualifications also listed on Georgia's announcements. Applicants with these competencies, education, or experience will usually be given first consideration in screening and hiring for that particular vacancy.[10]

Ranking

Once candidates are rated (i.e., qualified candidates are separated from those people who do not possess the minimum qualifications for the job in question), they must then be *ranked* to determine who are the best among them. These are the individuals who are referred to the selecting official for consideration and are the ones who usually get selected.

Candidates are generally ranked based on the KSAs required for the position being announced. The KSAs are critical to the ranking process because the premise behind ranking candidates is that people who score higher on these KSAs are more likely to be successful in that job than people with a lower score.

The federal government typically ranks candidates on a scale of 70 to 100, with 70 representing the lowest score for someone who meets the minimum qualification requirements for the job. Veterans' preference is then added onto each candidate's score, when appropriate.

Let's look at the KSAs for a job in the federal government. The Department of the Air Force, Air National Guard was recently looking for a motor vehicle operator. The announcement indicated that

> the following knowledge, skills, and abilities will be used to determine the best qualified applicants from which selection will be made:
>
> a.   Skill in operating gasoline or diesel powered trucks or trailer or semi-trailer coupled by use of a turntable (fifth wheel) or pintle (pivot) hook.
>
> b.   Skill in using two braking systems along with the gear shift controls.
>
> c.   Knowledge of and skill in the use of a turntable or pintle hook."

Either a staffing specialist or panel of one or more subject matter experts (SMEs) would rank the candidates and then assign a score to each. From the agency's perspective, the key goals would be to ensure that (1) it identified the right KSAs, (2) it developed an appropriate *crediting plan* (a crediting plan is an objective statement of position qualification requirements and criteria against which applicants are evaluated), and (3) it had a skilled and experienced person(s) to rank the candidates.

Not all ranking processes are the same, so let's look at a different one. In Ramsey County, Minnesota, they sometimes take a different approach. For the position of claims administrator, they rank applicants in the following manner:

> **EXAMINATION:** The screening/examination process will consist of the following sections with each section weighted as indicated.
>
> 1) Training and Experience Rating 30%
> 2) Oral Examination 70%
>
> *Note:* If 20 or fewer candidates pass the Training and Experience rating, 100% of the scoring weight of the test will be based on this rating and there will be no Oral Examination.[12]

Under Ramsey County's ranking system, an oral examination makes up the bulk of the evaluation, which is not the way that the federal government ranks applicants. I suspect that Ramsey County relies on oral interviews because it has relatively few vacancies as compared with the federal government, which as of this writing is recruiting for more than 41,000 vacancies. The advantage of Ramsey County's approach is that it is more personal and it allows the county to evaluate candidates on both the written material that they submit as well as on the way they respond to verbal questions. This provides interviewers with a much more three-dimensional view of applicants and allows the interviewer(s) to challenge some of the more questionable responses. In essence, this approach makes it less likely that one or more of the candidates will receive a skewed ranking by simply submitting a written application that contains information that is less than accurate.

On the other hand, Ramsey County will only use this method when more than 20 applicants apply, meaning in most cases it will revert to a model that more closely mirrors the federal government's approach.

Regardless of the way that a government agency chooses to rank candidates, it will eventually narrow down the pool of eligible applicants so that the selecting official has to interview only a manageable number of people, presumably those who are the best qualified for the job. The more precisely that an agency makes accurate distinctions between qualified applicants and the *best qualified applicants*, the more likely it will make the best possible selections.

Veterans' Preference

There is one other key component of the rating process and that is the assignment of veterans' preference to the score of each eligible candidate. Veterans' preference is a time-honored tradition at nearly every level of government. Veterans' preference "recognizes the economic loss suffered by citizens who have served their country in uniform, restores veterans to a favorable competitive position for Government employment, and acknowledges the larger obligation owed to disabled veterans."[13]

At the federal level, veterans' preference applies in hiring from civil service examinations conducted by the OPM and agencies under delegated examining authority . . . "and when agencies make temporary, term, and overseas limited appointments. Veterans' preference does not apply to promotion, reassignment, change to lower grade, transfer or reinstatement."[14]

The rules pertaining to veterans' preference do not mandate that an agency uses a specific appointment process. Federal agencies have the discretion to hire from many different sources (e.g., reinstating a former federal employee or reassigning a current employee).

Depending upon the category that they fall under, eligible veterans receive the following preference:

5-Point Preference (TP)
Five points are added to the *passing* examination score or rating of a veteran who served:

- During a war; or

- During the period April 28, 1952 through July 1, 1955; or

- For more than 180 consecutive days, other than for training, any part of which occurred after January 31, 1955, and before October 15, 1976; or

- During the Gulf War from August 2, 1990, through January 2, 1992; or

- For more than 180 consecutive days, other than for train-

ing, any part of which occurred during the period beginning September 11, 2001, and ending on the date prescribed by Presidential proclamation or by law as the last
day of Operation Iraqi Freedom; or

  ➢ In a campaign or expedition for which a campaign medal
      has been authorized."[15]

10-Point Disability Preference

Ten points are added to the *passing* examination score or rating of a veteran who served:

  ➢ At any time *and* who has a compensable service-
      connected disability rating of at least 10 percent but less
      than 30 percent (CP)

  ➢ At any time and who has a compensable service-
      connected disability rating of 30 percent or more (CPS)

  ➢ At any time and has a present service-connected disabil-
      ity or is receiving compensation, disability retirement
      benefits, or pension from the military or the Department
      of Veterans Affairs but does not qualify as a CP or CPS;
      or a veteran who received a Purple Heart.

  ➢ Ten points are added to the *passing* examination score or
      rating of spouses, widows, widowers, or mothers of
      veterans as described below. This type of preference is
      usually referred to as "derived preference" because it is
      based on service of a veteran who is not able to use the
      preference.

Veterans eligible for preference who meet the minimum qualifications
for a job have 5 or 10 extra points added to their rating depending on the
category of preference they fit into. This means their highest possible rating
is 110 (100 points being the maximum score possible for most people, plus
the 5 or 10 extra points granted to eligible veterans).

Those veterans with 10-point preference who receive service-connected
disability compensation from the U.S. Department of Veterans Affairs of 10
percent or more (CP and CPS) are listed at the top of the register in numerical order ahead of all other eligible candidates. The remaining veterans with

10-point preference, 5-point preference, and other candidates are listed in order of their scores. A veteran with preference is listed ahead of people who do not qualify for preference but who have the same score.[16]

Many state and local governments take a similar approach in granting veterans' preference. For example, Maryland offers veterans an eligibility credit when applying for jobs, as follows:

> An appointing authority shall apply a credit of ten points on any selection test for:
>
> 1. An eligible veteran;
>
> 2. The spouse of an eligible veteran who has a service connected disability; or
>
> 3. The surviving spouse of a deceased eligible veteran.
>
> An appointing authority shall apply a credit of two additional points on any selection test for:
>
> 1. An eligible veteran who has a service connected disability; or
>
> 2. A former prisoner of war.[17]

Conversely, for the city of Santa Clarita, in Southern California, I could not find any mention of veterans' preference for city jobs on its Web site.[18] Perhaps because it is a relatively small and new entity, the city has not yet added this to its hiring process. Regardless of the reason, the Santa Clarita example illustrates why it is nearly impossible to make broad, all-encompassing statements regarding the overall hiring process at the state and local levels.

Interviewing

Once the list of qualified candidates has been pared down and the selecting official receives a certificate of eligible applicants, it is time to begin the interviewing process. This is a crucial part of the selection process because this is the opportunity for the selecting official to put a face to the name and background of each person she will be considering.

The first step in this process is to contact all of the candidates and set up an interview. Typically, a letter is sent to each person asking them if they are still interested in being considered for the job in question. If they are interested, they are then advised to call a phone number to set up an interview. They are then required to return that letter to the agency and formally state whether they are interested in the job or not. The reason for this is to remove people from the list who are no longer interested in being considered for the job, so that management will know who to formally consider.

Preparation

Before interviewing each candidate, you must prepare for the interview. This means reviewing the application in advance and identifying any areas on the application that spark your interest—either positively or negatively. Do not wait until the interview begins to do this; otherwise, you may rush through the review process and miss a key issue that should have been pursued further.

In addition, if you wait until the interview to start reviewing the application, and then fumble around in a distracted manner, you can easily come across as being disorganized and unprofessional. Remember that the person you are interviewing is also interviewing you in order to determine if this is an organization he wants to work for. If you give him a negative impression, it may turn him off and he may decide to withdraw his application, even though from your perspective he may turn out to be an excellent candidate.

I strongly recommend that you prepare the same series of questions for each candidate prior to the interview. There are several reasons for this: If you wait until the interview to think up questions, you may ask the wrong ones or forget some important ones to ask. By having the same list of questions for each applicant, you will ensure that everyone is treated the same, which is always a key concern when selecting people for government jobs. Otherwise, you may open yourself up to an equal employment opportunities (EEO) complaint if an unsuccessful candidate learns that he has been treated differently than others.

Keep in mind that I am not recommending that you ask everyone the exact same series of questions because that would be too constrictive and unrealistic. Rather, I am recommending that you ask everyone the same initial questions and then follow up with questions based on the responses you receive.

In terms of the questions themselves, I suggest that you ask both a mix of open-ended questions as well as more detailed, job-specific questions. Examples of open-ended questions include the following:

> Why did you decide to apply for this particular job?
> What is your background?
> What are your career goals?

These are a starting point for learning something about the person you are considering for a job. They are intentionally open-ended in order to allow the person to answer in any way that he chooses. At the same time, they are precursors for the more detailed questions that you should ask after that.

If one candidate replies to your first question by stating that he wants to come to work for the government in order to have job security and a good set of benefits, and another indicates that he loves your mission and wants to make a difference, that tells you quite a bit about each candidate's motivation.

To use another example: If one individual states that he wants to work for the government for a while and then decide where to go from there, and another indicates that she wants to make the government her career because she feels that this is the best possible niche for her, this too tells you something about each candidate's motivation and allows you to make meaningful distinctions between the two. As you move forward in the interview, your remaining open-ended questions and your more job-specific queries will help to provide you with a good sense of the person in front of you.

More detailed questions should relate to the job analysis, which should have been completed prior to issuance of the vacancy announcement. The job analysis flows from the position description and lists the KSAs required for the job. The detailed questions are designed to tell you how well the candidate possesses those KSAs and to give you a chance to compare his skills relative with the competition.

Examples of additional talking points include:

➤ Describe your greatest strengths that relate to the job in question.

➤ Give several examples of problems that you previously encountered at work and explain how you solved them.

➤ Talk about several concerns that have been expressed to you by your previous customers and articulate what you did to allay them.

➤ Tell me about several creative ideas that you offered to your previous employers and explain why they were or were not implemented.

I recommend grouping your questions around each of the KSAs. In this way, there will be a logical flow to your questions and a strong nexus between the questions and the requirements of the job.

For example, if one of the KSAs involves writing skills, you might ask some of the questions listed below:

➤ What were some of the written materials that you prepared for your previous organizations?

➤ To what degree did others review these documents?

➤ What classes have you taken to improve your writing skills?

➤ Have you ever been called upon to review the writing of other employees? If so, why?

The point here is to ask a balanced mix of questions that will provide you with insight into the background, behavior, and thinking of the person you are considering for a job. After all, this is your best opportunity to get inside the head of the person in front of you and to figure out whether he will ultimately be an asset to your organization. If red flags appear (e.g., gaps in the person's resume or evasive answers to your questions), this is your best opportunity to clarify them. Remember, the more you can get behind the slick resume and canned answers that most people provide, the better you will be able to make an informed decision, which is the bottom line of the selection process.

The Interview Itself

Once the interview begins, try to create a positive atmosphere and put the applicant at ease. Smile, greet him, and shake his hand. Let him know that you are happy he is here and thank him for taking the time to come and meet with you. Exchange a few pleasantries in order to allow him to relax. Also, give him some information about the interview process and what you will be looking for. From the interviewee's perspective, it is always good to have some idea of what to expect.

Always conduct the interview in a private office or a secure space in order to allow for the most frank and open discussion possible. Prior to the interview beginning, it is always nice and appropriate to offer the applicant a glass of water or a cup of coffee.

Once the interview begins, ask your pre-developed questions in the order that you developed them; however, be prepared to ask follow-up questions any time they are in order. Try and stay within the time frame you have allotted for the interview, but be prepared to expand it a bit if you need to learn more about the candidate. On the other hand, if it is clear that the interview is not going anywhere, and you are not *required* to select the candidate (as in the case of a disabled veteran), and the applicant is a bad fit, do not extend it unnecessarily. Simply ask the minimum number of questions that you had identified, and then end the meeting. There is no need to waste your time or the time of the person you are interviewing.

Listen carefully to what the interviewee has to say and, by all means, take notes throughout the meeting. Do not rely exclusively on your memory because it is very difficult to recall everything that takes place during an interview. This is especially important if you are interviewing multiple candidates. Moreover, in the event that an EEO complaint is later filed, your notes may ultimately prove to be your only source of information, other than your recollection, for justifying your selection.

This is why I recommend developing an interview template for every interview. The template should list the name of each candidate, the job he or she is applying for, and the vacancy announcement number. It should also contain all of the pre-developed interview questions, space for follow-up questions, and room to jot down the gist of the candidate's responses. Last, it should have a section for notes, wherein you can list your key observations about each applicant (e.g., "He came late to the interview"; "He did not directly answer many of the questions, especially questions 1, 3, 5, and 6"; "Based on my review of his resume and the way he expresses himself, he appears to have very strong communication skills"; "He indicates that he doesn't like working with people"). The more detailed and specific you can be on this template, or in simply jotting down your observations on a piece of paper, the easier it will be for you to recall each candidate and to defend your final decision(s).

That having been said, it is also important to pay close attention to each applicant's body language during the interview because people communicate in many different ways, and body language is one of the best ways to learn about a person. If your candidate looks you in the eye, smiles, and gives you a firm handshake, that may be a sign of someone who has confidence in himself. On the other hand, if the candidate averts his eyes from you, gives you a weak handshake, and never smiles during the interview, that probably tells you that this is not a person who is overly confident.

As the interview progresses, if the candidate hesitates in answering your questions, speaks in doubletalk, or constantly downplays your follow-up questions, that may be a sign that he is trying to hide something. Conversely, if he answers each question with confidence and responds with specifics where he can but is not afraid to reply "I don't know" to certain questions, that is probably a good indication that this is a strong candidate who is worthy of serious consideration. It is important to pay rapt attention during the interview because it is simply your best chance to learn as much as possible about someone who may wind up working in your organization for 30 years or more.

Throughout the interview, remain as professional as you can. For example, do not offer your opinion on events that are unrelated to the job in question. There is no reason to discuss your feelings regarding an upcoming election or your stance on a controversial social issue, such as gay rights, abortion, or capital punishment.

Do not ask inappropriate questions of a personal nature; they may come back to haunt you. The following questions should not be asked because they delve into inappropriate areas of an applicant's personal life and they could get you into a lot of trouble:

> ➤   Are you married?
> ➤   Are you planning to have any children?
> ➤   How old are you?

> ➤ What political party are you affiliated with?

> ➤ What is your religion?

> ➤ Do you have any physical or mental handicaps?

In my experience, if an interviewer asks those types of questions, it could easily give an interviewee the impression that they will not be selected if they give the wrong answer(s). Even if they wind up being nonselected for legitimate, nondiscriminatory reasons, the damage would most likely already have been done, leaving the person(s) who was not selected with the sense that they were a victim of discrimination. This then could trigger a charge of employment discrimination based on prohibited reasons, which you would probably lose, based on the questions asked at the interview, and could very likely have an adverse impact on your career.

Take it from me: This is a battle you do not want to fight, so never give someone ammunition that could be used against you. Play it smart and keep your questions focused on the job and only the job and you will make things easier for everyone concerned.

At the same time, be careful not to fall into the trap of making a selection because you wind up liking the person you are interviewing. Sometimes when we interview individuals, we find that we have a lot in common with them and we establish a personal connection. This can be a good thing but it can also take you down a path that can ultimately be damaging to everyone.

Only select people who you think will be a good fit for the job in question based on as much objective evidence as is available. That is not to say that you should reject people that you like; you should not. But do not let a personal connection at the interview divert you from your mission, which is to select the best possible candidate for the job.

I recall a selecting official who hired a candidate because he was dazzled by the individual's personality. The official felt that this candidate had a tremendous amount of charisma and that his energy and enthusiasm would have a positive effect on the rest of the workforce. I was skeptical of his choice and felt that he should go with a different candidate who was less charismatic but who was a more solid, hard-working individual. Ultimately, I deferred to the official's judgment and allowed him to go with the person he liked. Unfortunately, we quickly learned that the candidate often got by on the force of his personality and did not delve into matters as deeply as we would have liked. In retrospect, we should have selected the second candidate, and we should not have allowed the first candidate's personality to cloud our collective judgment.

On the other hand, do not immediately dismiss candidates because you do not like them. Sometimes we form a negative impression about individuals simply because we don't like the way they dress, how they cut their hair, or their sense of humor. However, these are not legitimate reasons to write someone off. In fact, it is important to ensure that your organization has a good mix of people with different ways of thinking, different perspectives, and different ideas. This will guarantee that your organization does not fall into the trap of developing a "group think" mentality on all issues. When that happens, important perspectives get ignored and people do not speak up, resulting in the organization making decisions based on a narrow frame of reference. In the long term, this means that the quality of the decision making will decline.

Be especially cautious about interviewing and selecting someone you have become attracted to. If you aren't cautious, you will quickly find that other people will pick up on your behavior[19] and will scrutinize every action you take that involves this individual. Once sexual attraction is an issue in the selection process, it becomes more and more difficult to justify your actions and can easily lead you astray. Again, the single best way to handle all interviews is to treat each candidate the same way.

With that in mind, always remember that whenever you interview people for a job, you must know what to look for in advance. If you are looking for someone who has strong customer satisfaction skills, make sure that you focus on that element during the interview. Avoid letting the interview get out of hand because of an extraneous piece of information. For example, if you interview someone for a public contact position and find out that he used to play in the National Football League (NFL), do not spend much time on that part of his background unless he was involved in a lot of public contact while in the NFL. While it may be exciting to meet a former NFL player, that may not be relevant to the interview. If you spend most of the interview focusing on his football career, once the interview is over you may be no closer to knowing if he would be any good as a contact representative than you were prior to the interview. That is why you always want to keep your focus on the task at hand.

At the end of the interview, I recommend giving each person a score on the template I described earlier. I would use a scale of 1 through 4 for each KSA, with 1 representing the lowest score and 4 representing the highest. If you decide to weight the KSAs (e.g., KSA one is twice as important as KSA two), indicate that on the template before the first interview. Simply add up the scores. This will show you how each candidate ranked against each other based on their interview.

It is important to note that there is no legal requirement to do this. However, it is an excellent way of building fairness into the system while enabling you to size up each applicant relative to pre-established criteria as well as to each other. Moreover, these forms do not have to go into the selection file unless you chose to put them in there, although I would recommend that you retain them for your personal files at a minimum.

A good way to overcome some of the potential problems that may occur during the interview process is to have several management officials conduct the interviews rather than just one. By taking this approach, it is far less likely that someone will be selected or not selected for the wrong reason(s) because the ultimate decision will be based on the perspective of several people. If all of the officials interview every candidate, document their observations/rankings in the same way I described earlier, and make the selections based on how they rank against the KSAs, that would eliminate many of the pitfalls that could occur if only one person made the selections.

To both make the process work even better and create the appearance of fairness to the maximum extent possible, I strongly recommend that the interview team be composed of a diverse group of people. By this I mean men and women, and whites and nonwhites. By taking this approach, it sends the message that you are committed to selecting a workforce that closely mirrors the local labor pool. It should also make it more difficult for anyone to allege discrimination when the selection team is itself diverse.

Think about it this way: If you were an African American female who was interviewed but not selected by a team composed of all white males, you might very well feel that you were not given a fair shot. This may be because you felt as though a team of your peers, or at least a group of people who had experiences that were somewhat similar to your own, did not question you. However, if the team had an African American male and a Hispanic female interviewing you, you probably would have felt that you were given a reasonable opportunity to state your case. While you still would have been unhappy at not being selected, odds are that you would be less likely to be unhappy with and complain about the decision not to select you.

Another advantage to this approach is that when you participate with two other people in making selection decisions, you will be less prone to asking inappropriate questions or letting your biases show, if for no other reason than you know that your peers are watching you. While this may be a sad commentary on human behavior, taking this approach will help keep both you and the organization out of trouble, which is definitely a good thing. Moreover, it will help to ensure that all of the management officials on the selection team develop the right habits when going through future selection processes.

CHAPTER

4

POST-INTERVIEW
REVIEW/MAKING
YOUR DECISION

NOW THAT YOU HAVE GONE through the interviewing process, you still need to do several things before you make the final selection(s). First of all, after the interview has been completed, I recommend that you give each applicant the chance to spend some time in the area where she will be working if selected in order for her to get a feel for the job. Pair her with a journeyman, let her see what the job entails, and then give her the chance to pick the journeyman's brain and ask him as many questions as she wants to.

This exercise will provide the applicant with the opportunity to see what the job is really like. Otherwise, you may wind up selecting someone who thinks he is going to be doing one job when, in reality, he will be doing something very different, which means the person will probably start off his career unhappy and that is not a good way to begin. Moreover, by allowing each candidate to spend time at the worksite and to watch the job being performed, they will (1) get a sense of what the work entails, (2) get an accurate view of the physical plant, (3) see who their coworkers will be, and (4) determine if this is an organization that they really want to be a part of.

This is extremely important because the last thing you want is to go

65

through the recruitment process, make a selection, return the certificate of eligible candidates, have the selectee quit her current job and start working for you, train her, have to deal with her complaints about the job, and then have her resign after a few months. If this happens, you will have wasted a monumental amount of time, energy, and money, you will have nothing to show for it, and you will be back at square one.

To illustrate this point, let me tell you about an individual who applied for a job with the government as an accounts receivable analyst GS-06/07. He was initially found to be unqualified for the job so he complained about that determination. After several conversations with human resources management (HRM), he filed an appeal, which required a staffing specialist to review the determination a second time. This time, the staffing specialist decided that the candidate was indeed qualified. The chief of finance spent an hour interviewing the candidate and quickly selected him for the job. The candidate was not given the opportunity to see what the job entailed or to spend any time at the work site or with the current employees.

When the candidate was notified that he was selected but would have to start at the GS-06 level, he became upset, believing that he had been given the impression that he would start at the GS-07 level. Accordingly, he filed an informal complaint asking that he start at the GS-07 level. His complaint prompted several internal discussions about his situation before it was finally decided that he would have to start at the GS-06 level.

Having accepted the job, and wanting to work for the government, he reluctantly agreed to start at the lower level, but now he had a bad taste in his mouth. When he began work, he was shocked by nearly everything that he saw. He felt that the work site was abysmal, the employees were cynical and uncommitted, and the work itself was neither interesting nor challenging. In short, the job was nothing like he envisioned it would be. After about a month, he resigned from the government, disenchanted with the way he was treated. Moreover, at every opportunity, he shared his negative experience and poor impression with anyone who would listen.

Had management taken the time to give this individual a greater sense of what the job would be like, in all likelihood, the candidate would never have accepted the job offer. Had that happened, I think it is fair to say that everyone would have been both happier and better served.

Following Up with Previous Employers

Prior to making a formal commitment, you should first contact each of the candidates' previous employers in order to get another perspective about the people you might hire. The fact of the matter is that some people can put together top-notch resumes and can perform at interviews very well, yet wind up being "employees from hell." While you will hopefully identify these individuals during the interview, recognize that there are some candidates who are so good at masking their true personalities that you must contact their prior employers in order to avoid making a major mistake. Remember, people are always on their best behavior during job interviews, so be particularly leery about people who seem to be too good to be true; sometimes, although certainly not all the time, they are.

A good analogy is the dating world. You shouldn't want to marry someone because of one great date. You simply don't know enough about that individual to make a life-long commitment. Obviously, you don't have the time to interview and then constantly re-interview candidates until all facets of their personality come out. Therefore, the next best thing to do is to gain as much insight into their personality and previous performance as possible.

I suggest that you not only get in touch with their last employer, but that you also contact at least one or more employers *before* the most recent one. These employers will have more distance from the prospective employee and will probably be more honest and open with you.

Let me tell you a few stories to illustrate my point. One organization that I worked at was recruiting for a management analyst. The organization used a panel of three individuals to interview each candidate. One particular applicant absolutely dazzled the interviewing panel with his charms, good looks, and intellect. Even though he had a relatively thin resume, they decided to select him right away, and they did not make much of an effort to contact his previous employers.

Once he started working, many of the young female employees would mill around his desk, hoping to talk to him, as they, too, were charmed by his magnetic personality. However, it soon became apparent that this individual knew that he was charismatic and he tended to get by on his looks and personality. He put almost no effort into the job and he frustrated upper management to no end. After ignoring several counseling sessions from his supervisor, who advised the individual that he needed to apply himself more thoroughly to his job, the employee was terminated during probation.

Another employee who had worked in that same organization for a number of years suddenly filed an equal employment opportunities (EEO) complaint when he was not selected as a supervisory management analyst. His complaint surprised everyone because he did not seem to be the type of individual who would file a grievance just because he was not selected for a job. Because I had recently become the second-line supervisor of that activity, I decided to sit down with the individual and see what was bothering him.

After dispensing with the usual pleasantries, he quickly informed me that he felt that this was his last opportunity to get into management and that he was very upset that he had not been selected. I was taken aback by his comments and remarked that I did not understand why he believed that he would not have another chance to get into management. His response floored me. He said that he had been convicted of murder. He had served his time, but he didn't think that he would have another opportunity to become a supervisor. Stunned, I told him that I was unaware of his past and would have to look into the matter and get back to him.

I quickly ordered his official personnel folder, expecting to find that he had not declared his conviction in the appropriate space on the application.[1] However, after reviewing it, I was shocked to find out that he did declare his conviction and that the selecting official who brought him on board either never noticed this or chose to ignore it. Moreover, the selecting official obviously did not check with the man's previous employer (or custodian), which in reality was the Department of Corrections. Either way, much to my chagrin, we were apparently stuck with a convicted murderer because no one in management or HRM had taken the time to look into this man's background.

Eventually, the anger that had caused this man to kill another person came back to the surface, in the form of a constant series of complaints, coupled with outright insubordination, and we eventually fired him. However, throughout the removal process, we were concerned about his potential for violence, given his history. Although he did not resort to any violence, we spent an inordinate amount of time both dealing with and worrying about him because we had not taken the time to do our homework.

At another time, I was the director of a government organization when it came to my attention that one of our supervisors had literally made up a story about one of her subordinates. Specifically, the subordinate had previously filed several EEO complaints against the supervisor, so the supervisor decided to invent a story that this individual had stolen some items from the government. She did this as a ploy to fire an employee who had obviously gotten under her skin.

Unfortunately for her, the lies began to unravel, and we quickly realized that her story was a complete fabrication. We immediately took action to fire the supervisor; however, due to pressure by an unsympathetic U.S. Merit Systems Protection Board (MSPB) judge,[2] we eventually placed her in a non-supervisory position.

This employee recognized that her reputation within our office had been damaged and that it was time to leave, so she started looking for another job. Eventually, she was selected in, of all places, an organization that was charged with resolving EEO cases!

I was amazed that they selected her in light of her record and inquired into how this could have happened. I was not surprised to find out that her new organization had never contacted us to learn about her employment history. They were simply too busy. I strongly suspect that had they taken the time to make a few phone calls, they would have never selected this individual.

The good news here is that the employee learned her lesson, and to my knowledge, she actually became a good employee. However, to a large extent, that is beside the point. When you make selections for jobs, you are always rolling the dice because there are no guarantees that people who look good on paper or during an interview will turn out to be successful. That is why you need to learn as much as you can about an individual before making a formal commitment. There is simply no other way to increase your odds of success.

The Selection Itself

Once you have completed your background checks, it is time to make your selection(s). It is important to move as quickly as you can because you never know if the candidates you are considering are also interviewing with other organizations (both in government and the private sector). Odds are that if you take too much time, you will lose one or more of them to another employer. Moreover, the ones you probably will lose are the applicants you are most excited about because other organizations will probably see things the same way that you do and will try and hire them as quickly as they can.

It is always a good idea to let each person know at the end of the interview how long it will take before selections are made. Candidates who have been interviewed by you and who really want to work for your organization will tend to get antsy if they don't hear from you within a reasonable period of time, or when they don't know when a final decision will be made. Providing them with a realistic time frame and then sticking to it is fair to them and helps yourself.

As you begin to make selections, look at each candidate's background again, preferably with the interviewing team if you used one. Line the candidates up from top to bottom according to their ranking on the civil service certificate and then decide who is selectable and who is not. By this I mean, in the federal government, you can make a selection only from the top three candidates who are interested in the job. Moreover, you cannot pass over an eligible veteran with preference to select a lower-ranking eligible candidate without veterans' preference who has the same or lower score. Let's look at this issue in more detail.

The Rule of Three

Assume you are a selecting official in the federal government and receive a certificate of candidates—a list of people who are eligible to be selected for the position(s) in question[3]— for one vacancy, ranked as follows:

Candidate A – 97.5
~~Candidate B – 91.0~~   Not interested
Candidate C – 89.4
Candidate D – 87.0
Candidate E – 85.0
Candidate F – 84.0
Candidate G – 83.5
Candidate H – 81.0

Your first step would be to canvass each candidate to see who is interested. For this example, let's say that the responses to your inquiries indicate that everyone is still interested in receiving consideration except for candidate B. Accordingly, because there are no veterans on this list, you would be able to select candidate A, C, or D.[4]

If you had two vacancies, you would still have to make your first selection from A, C, and D. Assuming you selected candidate C, your second selection would have to be made from A, D, and E because they would now be the top three candidates who were available and remaining on the certificate. To illustrate that point, here is what that certificate would look like for the second vacancy:

Candidate A – 97.5

~~Candidate B – 91.0~~ Not interested

~~Candidate C – 89.4~~ Selected for first vacancy

Candidate D – 87.0

Candidate E – 85.0

Candidate F – 84.0

Candidate G – 83.5

Candidate H – 81.0

As you can see, candidates A, D, and E are now the top three candidates remaining, requiring the selecting official to choose from this group.

Rule of Three Considerations

According to the U.S. Office of Personnel Management (OPM) policy guidelines, "An appointing officer is not required to consider an eligible who has been considered by him for three separate appointments from the same or different certificates for the same position."[5] In other words, if the same candidate has been nonselected three times for the same job, he may be eliminated from further consideration for future vacancies. Let's see how this would apply in the above scenario, except we are now changing the number of vacancies from two to four.

So far, candidate C has been selected. For the second vacancy, candidate A is selected, meaning that the certificate will now look like this:

~~Candidate A – 97.5~~   Selected for second vacancy

~~Candidate B – 91.0~~   Not interested

~~Candidate C – 89.4~~   Selected for first vacancy

Candidate D – 87.0

Candidate E – 85.0

Candidate F – 84.0

Candidate G – 83.5

Candidate H – 81.0

For the third vacancy, we would have to select from candidates D, E, and F. Note that this would be the third time that candidate D has been considered for the same position. Assuming we go ahead and select candidate E, candidate D would then be eliminated from further consideration at the discretion of the selecting official due to the rule of three considerations. As such, here is how the certificate would look prior to the fourth selection:

~~Candidate A – 97.5~~   Selected for second vacancy

~~Candidate B – 91.0~~   Not interested

~~Candidate C – 89.4~~   Selected for first vacancy

~~Candidate D – 87.0~~   Eliminated—three considerations

~~Candidate E – 85.0~~   Selected for third vacancy

Candidate F – 84.0

Candidate G – 83.5

Candidate H – 81.0

For the fourth and final vacancy, the selecting official would select from candidates F, G, and H.

Veterans' Preference

The above scenarios are relatively simple to apply once you understand them. However, if there are veterans eligible for preference on the list, the decisions become a bit more complicated, as we shall see.

If you recall what I said earlier, you cannot pass over an eligible veteran with preference to select a lower-ranking eligible candidate without veterans' preference who has the same or lower score. Let's look at a couple of examples to illustrate this point.

In the first example, assume that we had the same list of candidates, but that candidate B was a 5-point preference eligible as shown below:

Candidate A – 97.5

Candidate B – 91.0 TP (Tentative Preference)

Candidate C – 89.4

Candidate D – 87.0

Candidate E – 85.0

Candidate F – 84.0

Candidate G – 83.5

Candidate H – 81.0

Under this scenario, you could only select either candidate A, whose score is higher than candidate B, or candidate B. You could not select anyone below candidate B because a selecting official may not pass over a person eligible for veterans' preference to select someone without preference, unless an objection has been sustained (more about that later).

In our second example, let's add one other person to the mix: a 10-point disabled veteran who automatically goes to the top of the list as follows:

Candidate A – 85.5 CP (Compensable Preference)

Candidate B – 97.5

Candidate C – 91.0 TP

Candidate D – 89.4

Candidate E – 87.0

Candidate F – 85.0

Candidate G – 84.0

Candidate H – 83.5

Candidate I – 81.0

Under this scenario, the selecting official may choose either of the veterans entitled to preference; however, she may not pass over the 10-point disabled veteran to select candidate B, unless an objection has been sustained.

Objecting to Veterans

An eligible veteran with preference can be eliminated from consideration only if the OPM sustains an objection to the veteran for adequate reasons. These reasons, which must be documented, can include medical disqualification, disqualification due to suitability, or other reasons. The OPM states:

> The following special provisions apply to disabled veterans with a compensable service-connected disability of 30 percent or more:
>
> ➤ If an agency proposes to pass over a disabled veteran on a certificate to select a person who is not a preference eligible, or to disqualify a disabled veteran based on the physical requirements of the position, it must at the same time notify both the Office of Personnel Management (OPM) and the disabled veteran of the reasons for the determination and of the veteran's right to respond to OPM within 15 days of the date of the notification.
>
> The agency must provide evidence to OPM that the notice was timely sent to the disabled veteran's last known address.
>
> ➤ OPM must make a determination on the disabled veteran's physical ability to perform the duties of the position, taking into account any additional information provided by the veteran.
>
> ➤ OPM will notify the agency and the disabled veteran of its decision, with which the agency must comply. If OPM agrees that the veteran cannot fulfill the physical requirements of the position, the agency may select another person from the certificate of eligibles. If OPM finds the veteran able to perform the job, the agency may not pass over the veteran.
>
> ➤ OPM is prohibited by law from delegating this function to any agency.[6]

Category-Based Ratings

The Human Capital Officers Act of 2002[7] gave federal agencies the authority to develop and institute a category-based rating method as an alternative way to rank applicants for positions filled through competitive examining. This approach allows agencies to assess outside candidates and then place them into two or more pre-determined categories.

The purpose of this approach is to enable an agency to choose from a greater number of candidates while preserving veterans' right to preference. Instead of ranking applicants by a numerical score and then selecting from the top three candidates, agencies assign eligible candidates to two or more groups based on pre-established, job-related criteria (e.g., "breadth and scope of competencies/KSAs; increased levels of difficulty or complexity of competencies/KSAs; successful performance on the job; and level of the job"[8]). Agencies then have the flexibility to select from among all the applicants in the highest-quality group without regard to the rule of three.

That having been said, veterans with preference who are assigned to a certain category receive absolute preference within their category. Thus, if a veteran with preference is in the category from which selections are being made, the selecting official may not select a nonveteran over the veteran unless the agency requests to pass over the veteran and the request is approved.

As you can see, this approach has its plusses and minuses just like every other approach. However, federal managers should recognize that it is one more tool in their toolbox and then use it when it makes sense for them.

At the state and local levels, the selection rules vary, with some organizations using a system that is close to or mirrors the federal government's,[9] and others using a system that is at least somewhat different. Let's take a look at a few examples that are different.

New York has its own rule of three. Under its system, all eligible candidates are given a ranking. Those at the highest score are immediately eligible for consideration for appointment. Candidates at lower scores can be considered only when there are fewer than three candidates at higher scores. Any candidate's eligibility for appointment is dependent upon his or her rank (all eligible candidates who received the same score are equally ranked) and the number of other candidates who are tied at that and higher-level ranks.

Scenario Number One

Score	Number of Candidates at This Score	Rank
100	1	1
95	1	2
90	1	3

Under this scenario, all three candidates at all three scores and ranks are equally eligible to be appointed.

Scenario Number Two

Score	Number of Candidates at This Score	Rank
100	10	1
95	10	11
90	10	21

Under this scenario, the 10 candidates at score 100 and rank 1 are the only people who are eligible for appointment. Should the number of candidates at 100 be reduced to 2 (e.g., if some get hired or if they decline consideration), then all 10 candidates at the score 95 (rank 11) can also be considered. The 10 candidates at the 90 score could be considered only if there were two or fewer candidates at the scores of 100 and 95 (ranks 1 and 11).[10]

The state of New Jersey handles the ranking process differently. When a certificate is issued from the list of eligible candidates, New Jersey's computer system numbers the relative "position" of each candidate on the certificate as a reference point for the agency doing the hiring. Certificates are issued using all active lists, with older lists positioned above newer lists. For example, an eligible ranked 10 on an old list may be ranked 1 on a certificate, and in addition, an eligible ranked 1 on a newer list may be 2 on the certificate. People who are tied in rank on a list are listed alphabetically, but they all occupy the same rank.[11]

Regarding veterans' preference in Kansas, most positions are open to external applicants but only state employees can apply for internal positions. However, an exception is made for veterans, who can apply for any position for which they meet the minimum qualifications, regardless of the type of posting. Moreover, any veteran who meets these eligibility requirements will be offered an interview for that vacancy when they meet certain conditions, but they are not guaranteed to be hired for the job.[12]

Meanwhile, in New Jersey, "in the open-competitive examination process, Disabled Veterans who pass the exam head the list in rank order, followed by veterans who pass the exam, then non-veterans."[13] This is one of the few times I found where a state or local government gave veterans even more rights than the federal government gave them.

Regardless of the system within which you are operating, the key is to first understand that particular system's rules, regulations, and nuances. Knowledge is power, and the more you know about your options, the more flexibility you will have and the better position you will be in to make a sound decision.

Do not fall into the mind-set that just because you work for the government, you cannot select good people. Although the government's systems certainly have constraints, recognize that they have been developed in the interests of fairness (e.g., the rule of three or being able to hire people with disabilities) or in order to recognize the sacrifices made by America's veterans. The more you understand the way that the system works and use that to your advantage, the better you will do.

Who to Select

Once you know who you can select, it is time to make your decision. If more than one person was involved in the interviewing process, they should also participate in the selection decision-making process.

The first thing to do is to gather as much information as you have about each selectable candidate. This should come from their resume and application, any transcripts you may have that document their education, all available notes from the interview, and reports from previous employers. The process should be as transparent as possible and, to the maximum extent within your control, free from patronage, favoritism, and discrimination.

Obviously, the goal is to select the best possible candidate for the job within the confines of the civil service system. However, that is not necessarily as easy as it sounds. After all, do you select someone who is grossly overqualified for a job while expecting him to leave once he gets a better offer, or do you go with the person whose qualifications are weaker but is much more likely to stay? Do you select a person who is the most experienced but seems too cynical, or do you take a chance on someone who is less experienced but is champing at the bit to come work for you?

The key is to make your selections in a logical and orderly fashion with the focus being on who will be the best fit(s) for the job being filled. If someone is an attorney or has a Ph.D., it does not necessarily follow that they will be the best person for the job you are looking to fill. What you want are people who possess the requisite KSAs for the job in question and whose backgrounds and personalities indicate that they will be the most likely individuals to succeed in the long term.

If you are looking for customer contact representatives, select individuals who have good people skills. If you are looking for someone to work in your security department, hire an individual who is stable and can handle difficult situations effectively.

Again, your selection should always be based on job-related criteria that have been (1) articulated on your announcement, (2) used in the rating and ranking process, (3) incorporated in your interview questions, and (4) listed on your applicant interview form, if you choose to use one. If you do all that, the selection process should be relatively simple because each step of the process would be consistent and simply build upon the previous steps.

A good way to check your decisions is to first try and explain them to yourself. If you can articulate internally the rationale behind each selection and nonselection, odds are you will be able to successfully defend your decisions to a complaining individual or third party. After all, even if someone disagrees with your decision, as long as you have an arguable rationale for your actions, you will rarely, if ever, get in trouble. You are much more likely to have problems, however, when you can't explain your rationale. When that happens, people often conclude that there must have been a hidden and nefarious reason for your decision because you are either unwilling or unable to explain your rationale.

Although odds are relatively low that most of your selection decisions will be challenged, especially if you develop the reputation as being a straight shooter, by getting into the habit of explaining them to yourself, you will hone your selection skills, feel stronger about your selections, and ultimately make better decisions.

Once the Selection Is Made

As soon as you have made your selections, call each selectee, congratulate them, and welcome them to your organization. Let them know the grade and step at which they will begin and give them a tentative starting date. Should a candidate be unhappy with his starting pay, this is the time to address that issue. Do not wait until you return the selection certificate and the new employee has quit his job and started working for you to deal with this. After all, if pay is going to be a source of aggravation, you need to know this before the employee comes on board. Moreover, keep in mind that if you are hiring multiple people and you adjust one individual's pay above the minimum rate, you may create dissension among the other hires. That is why it is essential to resolve the issue of pay, if it arises, up front.

In addition, if any medical or drug tests, background investigations, or other criteria are required for the job, let the selectee know that as well. You want to make sure that all collateral issues are brought to the selectee's attention before they report for duty.[14]

Once you have reached agreement, follow up your conversation with a formal letter. This will ensure that everyone is clear about the terms of employment.

If you are bringing on more than one individual to perform the same job, your best bet is to have them start on the same day. This way, they can all be trained concurrently, which is much easier from a logistical standpoint (e.g., training, communication, resources).

Orientation

Once the new employees start, it is always a good idea to provide them with a formal orientation to your organization. This is an opportunity to teach them about your organization, including its history, culture, and values. It is also an excellent time to process everyone's paperwork and to answer all of their questions about how and when they will get paid, their benefits, promotional opportunities, joining the union, and any special programs that you offer, such as leave donation or student loan repayments. It is also the perfect occasion to give a more detailed tour of your organization so they know where everything is located and they can find their way around.

I would like to make a few recommendations regarding the way you conduct the orientation. First of all, hold it in a location that is attractive and sends a message to the new employees that this is a government organization that values both its customers and its employees. Unfortunately, I have far too often seen new employees steered to a drab and unattractive location for orientation, which immediately sends a negative message to them on their first day of work. Remember, you have only one chance to make a strong first impression on new employees—take advantage of it. Find or develop a room that is bright and airy; that contains your mission, vision, and guiding principles; that proudly displays photographs highlighting your mission; and that celebrates the good work of your employees. Such a room will serve to reinforce the core values that you want to share with the employees during orientation.

Also, try and have your leader, or if she is unavailable then someone near the top of the organization, speak to the new employees. They deserve to know who is in charge, what she believes in, what the political forces currently are, and where the organization is going. Providing the employees with access to a local senior leader at the onset of their careers will show them that they are truly appreciated and it will also give them a valuable perspective on where they fit in the scheme of things.

Additionally, try and arrange for the employees to hear from the overall leader of the organization. This individual should give them a sense of the big picture and an understanding about where the organization is going.

Another helpful approach is to show a video, if available, that traces the history of your agency. Employees like to know where the organization came from and how it evolved.

It would also be wise to have a journeyman employee speak to the group to let them know what to expect, a union official to let the group know what the union offers, and an HRM specialist to oversee the entire session in order to ensure that all of the group's technical questions are answered.

In closing, you have just devoted an enormous amount of time, energy, and money to bring on one or more new employees. If you follow the strategies that I have outlined in this section of the book, I am confident that you will have a strong and diverse group of new employees who will serve you well in the years to come. Take some time to ensure that their initial experience is a positive one. It will be well worth the effort.

2

HOW TO FIRE A GOVERNMENT EMPLOYEE

CHAPTER

5

HANDLING POOR EMPLOYEES

WE JUST SPENT four chapters talking about how to hire government employees and now we have come to the flip side: how to fire them. As managers, we spend so much time trying to hire the right people you would think we shouldn't have to then fire some of them, but the reality is that sometimes we must. It may be because we made a bad choice or it may simply be that events occurred (either personal or professional) that changed the person and made him a less-than-productive employee. Regardless of the reason, odds are there is going to come a point where you should remove a bad employee. It is as simple as that.

You may not like to do this; in fact, nobody does. However, the cost of allowing a bad employee to linger in your organization can be astronomical. Maybe not right away, but as time goes by, other employees will get the message that poor performance or conduct is acceptable and some will begin to slow down. Others will start to behave in a less-than-optimal manner, and many of your best employees will leave—for the simple reason that they do not want to work for an organization that tolerates poor employees. Moreover, if supervisors also conclude that there is no point in dealing with problem employees because upper management will not support their decisions, they will stop taking action and simply sweep all of the problems under the rug, which will compound the problem even further.

Unfortunately, the perception and, to a large extent, the reality seems to be that government employees are invulnerable. That is what my friends in the private sector have told me and that is what I have heard from many less-than-satisfied colleagues in the public sector. They all believe that the government's personnel systems simply make it too difficult to fire an employee, which causes the government's supervisors to follow the path of least resistance (e.g., either looking the other way when someone performs or behaves poorly or moving the employee around without dealing with him).

The public perceives, at least to some extent, that government employees are lazy, are overpaid, have too much job security, and collect a pension that is disproportionately high when compared with the private sector. The following blog post is reflective of that perception:

> Let's fire every government worker from the smallest village receptionist or sewer worker to the staffers of the highest Senator and every menial clerk and recalcitrant paper shuffler in between.
>
> It's not just pique at the famous laziness of a government worker and it's not just the fact that the only reason they got their jobs is because they are pals with one politician or another. It's not just that they are better paid than just about any real American in the private sector—whether they deserve it or not—and it's not because they are impossible to fire, nor is it because they get a better pension and health care than anyone who *really* contributes to society . . . well, OK, it is because of that stuff. All that stuff and more.[1]

Unfortunately, far too many government employees seem to share this perception. For example, according to the U.S. Office of Personnel Management (OPM) 2007 annual employee survey, only 39 percent of the employees surveyed either strongly agreed or agreed to the following statement: "In my work unit, steps are taken to deal with a poor performer who cannot or will not improve."[2]

There are several reasons why so many people believe that poor government employees are not held accountable. The most obvious is that too many bad employees have been allowed to skate by and this lack of inaction has not gone unnoticed. I have certainly seen this throughout my career, as have many other government employees, the media, and people in the private sector.

The more important questions are why has this happened, and what can be done to change the way that the government holds its employees accountable? Let's examine each question in more detail.

Why Does the Government Not Deal with Poor Performers as Frequently as It Should?

One of the major differences between the public and private sector is that government employees have far more protection from losing their jobs than their counterparts outside of government. Let's take a brief look at how these protections developed.

History of Employee Protections in the Civil Service

As I described in Chapter 1, the modern civil service system can be traced to the Pendleton Act of 1883, which marked the beginning of the end of the spoils system and the establishment of the merit system for hiring federal employees. While the Pendleton Act changed the way in which many government employees were hired, it did not provide government employees any significant protections from unjust removals.

A breakthrough occurred on August 24, 1912, when in response to injustices to postal service employees during the Taft administration, Congress passed the Lloyd-LaFollete Act. This act "began the process of protecting civil servants in the United States from unwarranted or abusive removal by codifying 'just cause' standards previously embodied in presidential orders. It define(d) 'just causes' as those that would promote the 'efficiency of the service.'"[3] Prior to this act, there was no such statutory prohibition on the federal government's authority to remove a federal employee, and an employee could be discharged with or without cause for conduct. The act was passed after the Roosevelt and Taft administrations prevented federal employees from communicating with Congress without prior authorization.

The Veterans' Preference Act of 1944 provided veterans with notice and appeal rights in matters of employee discipline and removals. The act established that a veteran could not be removed, suspended, or demoted without good cause and without first receiving written notice of the charges, an opportunity to respond, and thirty days' notice. The veteran then had the right to appeal his termination to the Civil Service Commission.

Another major change occurred in 1962 when President Kennedy issued Executive Order 10988, which established a uniform set of policies on labor-management relations that for the first time applied to all departments and agencies. Prior to that, although unions had existed for many years, the federal government did not have a consistent set of policies for dealing with them.

Kennedy's order reiterated the importance of employee participation in the development of personnel policies, declared that employees have the right to join or not to join unions, and required that management negotiate with unions on a variety of issues.

That same year, Executive Order 10987 gave nonveteran employees the same appeal rights that the Veterans' Preference Act of 1944 had established for veterans. The order required all federal organizations to establish internal appeals procedures enabling employees to request an internal review of proposed adverse actions before appealing to the Civil Service Commission. From that point on, nearly all federal employees had the right to appeal such actions as removals and suspensions to the Commission.

According to the OPM,

> The Intergovernmental Personnel Act of 1970 substantially increased the role of the Federal Government in advancing merit systems of employment at the State and local levels. The Social Security Act amendments in 1940 required State and local governments to establish merit systems in their agencies that would receive Federal grants under various programs. Over time, the requirements for merit systems extended to additional grant programs of other Federal departments and agencies.[4]

In 1972, Congress enacted the Equal Employment Opportunity Act, which directed the Civil Service Commission to bring the federal civil service into line with the precepts of equal employment opportunity (EEO). Subsequent amendments to the act

> created the Equal Employment Opportunity Coordinating Council (EEOC), composed of the Civil Service Commission, Equal Employment Opportunity Commission (EEOC), and the Departments of Labor and Justice. The EEOC took on the task of trying to create a single set of employment guidelines that would provide consistent selection guidance to employers, both private and public. The basic premise of the guidelines was that employers could not use any employment selection procedure that had an adverse impact on any ethnic or racial group.[5]

Six years later, Jimmy Carter signed the Civil Service Reform Act of 1978, which abolished the Civil Service Commission and established the OPM in its place. The act also established the Federal Labor Relations Authority (FLRA) to oversee the federal government's labor relations program and the U.S. Merit Systems Protection Board (MSPB), which adjudicated employee appeals. One significant component of the MSPB included the special counsel, which became responsible for investigating and prosecuting charges against a federal official for violating the merit system.

The Civil Service Reform Act also transferred responsibility for equal employment opportunity to the Equal Employment Opportunity Commission (EEOC). The EEOC "assumed responsibility for enforcing anti-discrimination laws applicable to the civilian federal workforce as well as coordinating all federal equal employment opportunity programs."[6]

One of the features of the act was to make it easier to deal with problem employees. For example, it clarified the grounds for taking action against poor performers or employees who committed misconduct. It also reduced the grounds for appeals of adverse actions that had built up over time.

For example, prior to the act, employees had to go through several levels of appeals on certain actions, and it took a long time for appeals to move through the system. The new act provided that those issues eligible for appeal could go only to the MSPB, where specific timelines were imposed for resolving appeals.

Under the old system, employees could file appeals on many grounds that went beyond actions for poor performance or misconduct. For example, employees often appealed a reduction in rank, meaning that they believed that management had reduced their rank or stature within their organization. The new act eliminated these types of appeals and restricted appeals to primarily adverse actions stemming from unacceptable performance or conduct.

The act also made it easier to remove poor performers. It accomplished this by requiring agencies to prove a performance-based case only by substantial evidence ("that degree of relevant evidence which a reasonable person, considering the record as a whole, might accept as adequate to support a conclusion, even though other reasonable persons might disagree"[7]), whereas in any other case (e.g., misconduct), an agency would have to prove its case by a preponderance of the evidence ("The degree of relevant evidence that a reasonable person, considering the record as a whole, would accept as sufficient to find that a contested fact is more likely to be true than untrue"[8]), which is a higher standard.

In 1989, Congress passed the Whistleblower Protection Act, which was designed to protect federal whistle-blowers. This legislation amended the Civil Service Reform Act and made it easier for whistle-blowers to prove retaliation, and it required corrective action whenever whistle blowing was a contributing factor in a challenged personnel decision.

The Whistleblower's Act also made the special counsel independent from the MSPB and made the special counsel responsible for protecting federal employees, who believed that they suffered retaliation for blowing the whistle on wrongdoing in their agencies. It enabled whistle-blowers to take their cases to the MSPB and seek corrective action.

Under President Clinton, reinventing government was implemented through the National Performance Review (NPR). One of its chief objectives was the abolishment of the Federal Personnel Manual (FPM), which many had long viewed as inhibiting management from taking appropriate action. However, the NPR did not change the basic procedures that federal managers had to follow in order to take performance- or conduct-based action, so it did not have any real effect in those areas.

Clinton also instituted an executive order mandating that there be labor-management partnerships within the federal government. However, that was subsequently revoked by President George W. Bush.

State and local governments have also evolved in this area, with many of their employee protection programs being similar to those of the federal government's. Of course, given the sheer size, scope, and diversity of these government entities, it would be impossible to provide a broad history of all the individual programs in this book. However, it is fair to say that most of them offer protections that are, at a minimum, more liberal than those offered to employees in the private sector.

For example, in the state of Delaware, the accountability procedures are quite extensive. Disciplinary actions, including removal, are only to be taken for just cause. As the state defines it, "'Just cause' means that management has sufficient reasons for imposing accountability. Just cause requires: showing that the employee has committed the charged offense; offering specified due process rights specified in this chapter; and imposing a penalty appropriate to the circumstances."[9]

Where appropriate, supervisors are encouraged to first give a written reprimand for specified misconduct, or where a verbal reprimand has not produced the desired effect. Prior to the issuance of a removal, suspension, or demotion, the employee is entitled to be notified in writing of the proposed action and the reasons behind it. Employees also have a right to a pre-decision meeting in these types of cases. Pre-decision meetings are informal meetings that are designed to provide employees with the chance to respond to the proposed action and explain why the proposed action is not justified or is too severe.

Delaware employees who have been terminated, demoted, or suspended may appeal this action within 30 days.

An example at the local level is St. Paul, Minnesota. Its policies, while somewhat similar to the federal government's, contain far less guidance and provide management with more flexibility. This is not surprising; I would expect that the larger the government entity, the greater the need for more bureaucracy and detailed procedures.

In St. Paul,

> when an appointing officer has good reason to believe that any employee has given cause for their reduction, either in rank and/or compensation, or for discharge, the appointing officer shall notify said employee, in writing, served person-

> ally or through the mail, at the employee's last known
> address, setting forth the charges against the employee. A
> copy of this communication shall, at the same time, be filed
> with the Office of Human Resources. Suspensions may be
> issued verbally.[10]

The city lists 22 potential causes for an employee's discharge, reduction, or suspension, but it does not provide much more guidance beyond that in its personnel policy manual.

An employee who has an adverse action taken against him is entitled to appeal that action to St. Paul's Civil Service Commission.

Regardless of your level, nearly all governments have extensive policies and procedures for removing employees, with the largest entity, the federal government, generally requiring its supervisors to jump through the greatest number of hoops. Government supervisors have to be careful to follow the procedures that have been set forth in their organization in order to have a removal sustained by a third party. However, in my experience, these procedures, while complex and relatively time-consuming, are not the real problem. If you understand how and why they are designed, follow the appropriate processes, utilize the correct strategy, and work with a skilled human resources management (HRM) specialist, you should prevail in the vast majority of cases. The remaining chapters in this book will show you how to make that a reality.

Perhaps the biggest roadblock to terminating a poor employee are the employee protections that have been built into the system. Poor employees use these protections (e.g., EEO complaints, grievances, reasonable accommodations, Unfair Labor Practice [ULP] charges, workers' compensation, the special counsel of the MSPB), which are well intended and based on specific needs, to tie management up in knots and place it, instead of the employee, on the defensive. By using the "best defense is a good offense" strategy, poor government employees have historically used their legal rights to grind management down and make them give up the fight rather than invest all of the requisite time, energy, and expense that is generally required to win a case.

Working the System

Let me give you an example of how this scenario often plays out in government. An employee frequently comes to work late. The supervisor finally confronts her and orally counsels her about her tardiness. She turns around and files a grievance, alleging that she is being treated unfairly. The supervisor now has to discuss this matter with HRM, respond to her grievance, and explain to upper management why one of his employees is filing a grievance.

The next time she is late he gives her a written counseling. She responds by filing a second grievance and alleges that her supervisor is retaliating against her for exercising her right to file the initial grievance. Her second-level supervisor, in order to avoid making waves, decides to settle the two grievances and put the matter to rest by reducing the written counseling to an oral one, which sends two messages: (1) The employee sees that management would rather settle than stand up to her and (2) the first-line supervisor sees that he is not going to get a lot of support from upper management.

The next time she comes in late, the supervisor decides to give her an admonishment. She responds by filing still another grievance and this time informs her supervisor that she has been appointed as a union steward and will require up to eight hours of official time per week to represent the bargaining unit, as per the local contract. Now the supervisor has still another grievance to deal with, plus he will lose her services for as much as a day or a week, not counting the time she will also spend pursuing her grievances.

She again comes in late and this time her supervisor gives her a reprimand. She responds by filing an EEO complaint, alleging that management is discriminating against her because she is a woman. Moreover, the union files a ULP charge, alleging that management is retaliating against her because of her union activities. At this point, the supervisor will have to deal with her prior grievances, an EEO counselor, and the FLRA, not to mention his supervisors, who are wondering what the hell is going on. Meanwhile, the employee will spend even more time away from the job as her grievances, EEO complaint, and the union's ULP charge are being adjudicated.

As you would expect, the employee comes in late again and this time the supervisor convinces upper management to propose her suspension. She files another EEO complaint and the union files a second ULP, with both alleging that she is a victim of retaliation for exercising her legal employee rights. She also alleges that she is now handicapped due to the stressful environment that her supervisor has created. The supervisor will now have to deal with all of the new charges plus look into her claims that she is a qualified handicapped employee and needs reasonable accommodation. Naturally, she will now require even more time to pursue all of these new complaints.

The employee comes in late yet another time and now upper management agrees with the supervisor to propose a longer suspension. She files still another EEO complaint and the union files an additional ULP, again claiming that she is a victim of retaliation. Meanwhile, she provides management with a doctor's note indicating that she is suffering from extreme stress, and she files a claim for workers' compensation and informs management that she will be out of work for an extended period of time due to her occupational illness. She also files a complaint with the special counsel of the MSPB, alleging that management has committed one or more prohibited personnel practices against her.

She finally returns to work, comes in late yet again, and this time management proposes her removal. During this seemingly never-ending ordeal, her supervisor has had to deal with three grievances, three EEO complaints, three ULPs, a complaint to the MSPB, a workers' compensation claim, and the fact that she has also become a union steward. Of course, he is still responsible for the work of his unit, which has suffered because he has been so focused on dealing with her situation and the unit has been divided as a result of the brouhaha that this employee has created. Still, the supervisor has tried to do the right thing and deal with the employee in the way that he has always been taught—by the book.

Finally, he can see the light at the end of the tunnel, believing that the employee is about to be terminated. Unfortunately, he then learns that the deciding official wants to give her another chance and is going to reassign her to a different unit. While he is pleased to personally be rid of her, he is both angry and frustrated that all of the time that he has put into this case has been for naught and that this employee will get another chance to wreak havoc in a different unit. Meanwhile, several messages are being sent through this particular organization as a result of this outcome: (1) The supervisor wonders why he should ever try firing another employee if all he is going to get is a lot of grief, look stupid in front of his subordinates and coworkers, and not be supported in the end; (2) other supervisors are going to think twice before going down this same path; and (3) some employees are going to be emboldened to slack off because they see that management is not serious about dealing with poor employees.

If you think the above example is extreme, think again. This is a realistic depiction of what happens every day in government and these lessons keep spreading and spreading and create more and more inaction. That is not to say that people do not get fired in government—they most certainly do. However, that is more the exception than the rule and that is why there is a widespread belief that it is almost impossible to fire a government employee.

Too many government managers have concluded that it is simply easier either to sweep problems under the rug or to move the problem employee around rather than to deal with him or her. They have either reached this conclusion based on their own personal experiences or on what others have told them; and what drives their mind-set are horror stories such as the one I just described. Managers honestly believe that it is simply too hard to fire a problem employee and that, even if they try, they will only get burned in the end. To put it a different way, managers choose to take the path of least resistance, which is inaction, instead of the much harder but ultimately more rewarding path of actually dealing with the problem up front.

What Can Be Done to Change the Way That the Government Holds Its Employees Accountable?

As you can see from the example cited above, the government's system of employee protections can sometimes be used to frustrate supervisors from taking action against problem employees. To some extent, that is the cost of doing business. However, there are strategies that can be used to minimize the impact of employees who use these protections to insulate themselves from management action. I will touch upon them shortly.

Before I do, I want to say that, for the most part,[11] there is absolutely no reason why government managers cannot and should not take action against bad employees, up to and including removal. The systems for terminating employees, whether for conduct, performance, or both, are simply not that difficult to either follow or administer. They require that management (1) follow some basic rules and procedures (e.g., access to documentation, time frames, or the right to reply to a higher official); (2) prove its case by either a preponderance of or substantial evidence, as appropriate; (3) establish a nexus, or connection, between the offense and the action taken and then show why it will promote the efficiency of the government; and (4) demonstrate that the penalty chosen is reasonable.

None of this is rocket science and a layperson can easily understand it. The rest of this book will cover all of these topics in sufficient detail to show you that removing government employees is not that difficult. You will learn that the problem is not the government's accountability systems; they are pretty straightforward and easy enough to work with. The real problem is the way that government managers *apply these systems.*

Obviously, the employee protections built into the system do not make things easy for someone trying to do his job and remove a poor employee. That will always be a bit of a challenge. Moreover, given that these protections are there to prevent employees from being mistreated, as many undoubtedly have been in the past, on balance the protections are a good thing for an open society such as ours.

People simply have to realize that while the system of protections sometimes offers challenges, any enlightened supervisor who follows the rules and procedures set forth within their organization, adopts the strategies outlined in this book, and finds a good HRM specialist to advise them throughout the process can overcome the challenges.

So how do you apply your overall accountability system in such a manner that poor employees are successfully dealt with? To me, it comes down to several key elements: (1) your organization's mind-set; (2) the skill and abilities of your management team, including your advisors; (3) your overall strategy for dealing with poor employees; and (4) weeding out problem employees during probation. Let's look at each element in more detail.

Your Organization's Mind-Set

In good organizations, management believes that bad employees must be dealt with and it is prepared to fire them when necessary. That is the organization's mind-set. I know that this seems simple and a bit obvious, but remember the results of the 2007 OPM survey wherein only 39 percent of the employees felt that in their unit steps were being taken to deal with a poor performer who cannot or will not improve. This point has been repeatedly hit home to me whenever I conduct a supervisory training class. Unfortunately, a large number of the supervisors who attend my classes complain that their senior managers either do not want to or cannot deal with problem employees.

To me, if the people at the top of an organization are not prepared to deal with difficult issues, that mentality is going to permeate quickly throughout the entire organization. Everyone will get the message that poor performers are valued and that management is not serious about excellent performance. Once that happens, it can have a devastating effect.

For example, I once took over an organization that never removed anyone. It seems that my predecessor equated firing a government employee to capital punishment, and he didn't believe in capital punishment. The net result was that for all intents and purposes, the supervisors had stopped trying to manage poor performers and the organization's overall performance suffered.

I quickly let everyone know that I expected the mind-set to change. Effective immediately, we were going to deal with poor performers and, if necessary, fire them, assuming they would not or could not improve. Of course, I had to provide the supervisors with a lot of training on how to deal with poor performers and why it was so important to do so. Fortunately, the supervisors came around pretty quickly and within a few months, I fired the person who everyone agreed was our worst employee. I then walked around and gauged the reaction of our employees to this new development and was heartened to learn that most of them were relieved and felt that it was about time that management dealt with a coworker who didn't pull her weight.

As time passed, other employees were also terminated. Everyone got the message that our organization now valued high performance, and our productivity, accuracy, and customer satisfaction all improved.

Before I go forward, I want to emphasize that the goal is never to fire a poor employee; the goal is always to turn him or her around. Managers invest so much time, energy, and money in training an employee, that to fire that person is never a victory; it is a defeat. That having been said, there are times in our careers when we have no other reasonable alternative but to fire a bad employee. When that happens, the organization must unite behind and support the supervisor who is doing the right thing.

If that happens, and everybody gets the message that management is ready, willing, and able to consistently deal with problem people, then several things will happen, all of which are good: (1) The lower-level supervisors will understand that management wants them to deal with performance problems and will stand behind them if they have a good case; (2) the top employees will become encouraged because they will see that management is serious about developing a top-notch organization; (3) the middle 80 percent will recognize that excellent performance will be recognized and that poor performance will not be accepted, which will prompt many people to try and improve; and (4) the worst employees will see that if they don't pick things up, they are likely to be fired, so they will intensify their efforts to improve.

All of this will happen if the organization simply develops the right mind-set.

The Skills and Abilities of Your Management Team

To maintain a strong accountability program, you need to make sure that your management team is properly trained on all aspects of discipline and performance management. This includes familiarizing them with the key rules, regulations, and procedures (e.g., the Code of Federal Regulations, your internal agency policies, the union contract) that apply to these areas.

When I refer to the management team, I am referring to everyone from the leader on down. Each management official must be absolutely committed to dealing with employee problems; otherwise, your accountability program will only be as strong as its weakest link. The leader must lead by both word of mouth and example. She must encourage her subordinate supervisors to take action when appropriate, but then must be prepared to back them up when the facts support them.

The division or service chiefs must take the same approach and be willing to support lesser actions (e.g., an admonishment) and propose stronger ones (e.g., longer suspensions, demotions, and removals). At the same time, the division or service chiefs need to help develop the first- and second-line supervisors so they are willing and able to do the right thing.

The lower-level supervisors deal with the day-to-day employee problems and they need to address these problems as soon as possible. Otherwise, these problems will slowly but surely metastasize throughout the unit and beyond, and delaying will only make problems that can usually be addressed fairly easily at the beginning infinitely more difficult to deal with in the long run.

All of your supervisors should go through the traditional 40-hour introduction to supervision class. This class is a valuable opportunity for them to learn the basics of supervision, and most classes are heavily weighted toward HRM. The supervisors should also attend more sophisticated classes on discipline and performance management, which will provide them with a stronger knowledge base. Such classes should contain key decisions of the third party that adjudicates your adverse actions (e.g., MSPB for the federal government, state civil service commissions, etc.).

When I was serving as the government's representative at third-party hearings, I often had one of our supervisors assist me, simply because this was a completely foreign world to this individual. I wanted him to watch how both sides prepared for the hearing, see how evidence was introduced, learn when and how objections were made, understand why the judge ruled the way he did, and grasp some of the key case law.

I knew that once he saw the process unfold, it would demystify things for him, and he would lose some of the fear of third parties that government officials often develop. Moreover, I felt that he would learn many valuable lessons, such as the importance of documentation, the need to develop a clear rationale for his actions, and the ability to demonstrate that he was treating his employees fairly and equitably. Last, I believed that by attending these hearings, he would gain more confidence in himself and the process and he would be much more likely to deal with a problem employee head on.

Because we couldn't possibly have every supervisor attend these hearings, we also held mock ones. The purpose of these mock hearings was to create a realistic scenario wherein some of the supervisors would have to testify about their actions and then be cross-examined by a skilled HRM specialist. While this was happening, the remaining supervisors were observing the hearing and acting as judges. At the end of the hearing, we would have the acting judges explain which side they would find for and why. This gave them the chance to take a step back and analyze the strengths and weaknesses of the cases that they often have to deal with.

As a group, we also discussed how each witness performed. We talked about who was credible and who was not and why, and I often explained to them what each witness could have done to come across better. (I will discuss how to prepare for a third-party hearing in much more detail in Chapter 8.) These experiences were invaluable and helped strengthen and mature our supervisory staff.

While you are training the supervisors, it is also essential that you inculcate into them the importance of dealing with problem employees. They absolutely need to understand that the organization is both behind them and counting on them to manage employee performance and behavior. They also have to learn the consequences for both the organization and themselves if they do not take appropriate action—a likely diminution of performance, and all the bad things that happen as a result of that.

Your Advisors

The other key players in building an excellent accountability program are the people who advise or represent management on employee adverse actions: HRM and your attorneys.

The HRM folks are the ones who hold management's hand throughout the process and who advise them on what they can and cannot do. These are your technical experts who can either be facilitators or inhibitors of your accountability program. Unfortunately, in my experience, far too many HRM "experts" spend most of their time finding reasons why management should not or cannot take action against a problem employee. It may be because these "experts" are inexperienced, have never attended a third-party hearing, or are just plain scared of losing a hearing and somehow being blamed for the loss.

I believe that the quality of HRM advisors declined precipitously during the Clinton administration when its reinventing government initiative caused many agencies to centralize HRM in order to save resources. While that certainly happened, it also devalued HRM as a career field and the number of sites having their own HRM staff plummeted. People stopped seeing HRM as an important career, and many advisors retired or simply left the field. Many of the remaining HRM employees often wound up in centralized sites, classifying and filling vacancies, with the number of skilled HRM advisors dropping at an alarming rate.

If your organization does not have strong and experienced HRM advisors upon whom you can rely, I encourage you to either find them elsewhere or, more likely, build them. This is more difficult than it sounds because the pool of such people in the government is so limited. A good way to address this issue is to use one or more retired HRM specialists who have a solid track record in this area to help develop and mentor the HRM staff that supports you.

The attorneys who represent you can also be problematical. First of all, they are not trained HRM specialists. As lawyers, they tend to look at an adverse action in terms of whether the government will be able to prevail before a third party. As such, they usually nitpick a case, identify all of its weaknesses, and encourage management to either settle the case or withdraw their action altogether.

Conversely, a good HRM advisor will look at a case from the perspective of whether or not taking action will help the organization and promote the efficiency of the service. Obviously, they also need to weigh how winnable the case may be and they should be advising the official who wants to take action on how to make the case as strong as possible. However, the HRM advisor's first goal should be to ensure that they are supporting management in meeting its objectives.

Another problem with attorneys is that they are often so busy with other legal matters (e.g., tort claims) that they simply don't have the time to properly represent management. When that happens, they usually push the organization to settle, which in many cases sends a message to the employees that if they stand up to management, they will do okay.

Throughout my career, I fought with many of the attorneys who represented my organization because, according to them, we never seemed to have a case we could win. While most people simply went along with their advice, I fiercely resisted it because I had already represented the government on multiple hearings, understood HRM far better, and knew that most cases were eminently winnable. Most of the attorneys eventually came to see things my way, but not without a struggle. I had to explain what was involved in managing an organization and why it was so important to move forward on many cases.[12] However, once they started working with me, instead of against me, attorneys became powerful allies in dealing with problem employees.

Your Overall Strategy for Dealing with Poor Employees

To me, this should be simple, but for whatever reason, many if not most government organizations seem to struggle with this one. Simply put, I developed three core strategies that aided me well throughout my career: (1) Identify your problem employees and design a strategy for dealing with each of them immediately; (2) when you have a problem, bring it to a head; and (3) in the case of discipline, when you are dealing with a poor employee, take as strong an action as you can to change the employee's behavior. Let's look at each strategy in more detail.

Identify Problem Employees

You know who your problem employees are. In fact, everybody in the immediate work unit knows who they are. There simply are no secrets among people who work closely together. That having been said, until you put a plan in place to deal with these people, they will plague you and undermine the performance of your organization. It is that simple. Unfortunately, far too many supervisors feel that if they wait long enough, the problem will somehow magically go away. While that occasionally will happen, because someone may retire or move on, odds are not in your favor. After all, who would want to hire these poor performers?

You need to take action that will either change the person or *change the person*. Either outcome is acceptable. What is not acceptable is maintaining the status quo because that poor employee is undermining your organization in ways that I have already described.

The first and best way to change the employee is to find out the root cause(s) of her problem(s) and mutually explore ways in which she can improve. For example, you may find that there have been some gaps in her training, she may need reasonable accommodation, or she may be experiencing some personal problems that require professional counseling. This is the classic "carrot" approach, which is designed to turn the employee around in as positive a way as possible.

However, if that won't work, and it usually doesn't for a chronically poor employee, then you need to use "the stick." By this I mean you should firm-ly advise her that if she doesn't become a productive employee, action will be taken to change her behavior or performance, up to and including her removal. In my experience, the only time that chronically problem employ-ees ever change is when they conclude that their jobs are truly in jeopardy.

The strategy that you use to deal with your problem employees should be based on the facts in each case and developed in conjunction with a strong HRM advisor and upper management. For example, you may have one person who has always been a problem but has never even been coun-seled. In his case, issuing him a letter of counseling that outlines all of his past transgressions and advises him that future instances of similar behavior will not be tolerated may be the right approach. This is because you are both drawing a line in the sand and painting a picture of his work history that eventually may help justify a removal in the event that you go down this path and the case goes to a third party.

On the other hand, you may find that you have already taken several light disciplinary actions against someone, without success, and that it is now time to take a much stronger approach. At a minimum, this will cer-tainly get that individual's attention.

The point here is that if you are determined to change a poor employee, it is best to have a plan. Otherwise, if you do not know where you are going, you will probably never get there.

I successfully used this approach throughout most of my career. For example, I recall a time when a division chief approached me and glumly stated that his division of close to two hundred people would never perform up to expectations unless we got rid of his problem employees. I asked him to give me a list of these individuals and I was surprised to see that it con-tained 29 names.

We discussed why each person was a problem and we crafted a strategy to deal with every one. The first component of the strategy was honesty; we wanted them all to know that we considered them to be problem employees and we tried to work with them to identify the root causes of their deficien-cies. Where appropriate, we issued performance improvement plans, disci-plinary/adverse actions, or letters of counseling. We did not move people around for the sake of giving them a fresh start.

Two years later, 23 of those employees had left the organization through removal, resignation, or retirement. The remaining six became productive employees. The division, which historically had experienced timeliness problems, achieved 13 out of 13 timeliness goals.

Bring the Problem to a Head

You may wonder what I mean when I say if you have a problem, bring it to a head. Simply put, I mean that the sooner you bring a problem out into the open, the sooner a solution will appear. As long as problem employees think you are not serious and that they are invulnerable, they will continue to go about their business without a care in the world—while you will be up at night wondering what to do about them.

Under that scenario, they will not change, because there is no reason for them to change. You are continuing to do things the way you have always done them, so why would you expect the results to be different?

The best way to solve the challenge of a problem employee is to stop pussyfooting around. You need to make it very clear to them that you are not the stereotypical government manager who cannot or will not deal with unacceptable conduct or performance. You then need to follow your words with actions, meaning taking an action whereby the employee's job is suddenly on the line and for the first time he realizes that he could actually lose it.

Many organizations that assist people in overcoming addiction use this same strategy. They have learned that addicts must first be brought down before they can be built up again. In a sense, many of these problem employees are addicts, too, because they have become addicted to misbehavior or poor performance and either cannot or will not change their ways.[13] However, once the employees are put in a position where they realize that they could lose the most secure job in the world, a government job, anything can happen.

For example, a division chief proposed the removal of an employee who was obviously very angry and troubled and who had been causing all sorts of problems. In my view, this was an unusually weak case because there was little documentation to back it up. When the employee met with me to give his reply to the proposed removal, I could see that he really didn't want to work for our organization and that he was looking for an exit strategy that wouldn't hurt him. It was also clear that he didn't want a removal from the government on his record and that he was scared of the consequences. We quickly agreed that it was in everybody's best interest that he leave our organization and we negotiated a deal whereby he applied for disability retirement. His application was subsequently approved.[14] This had a positive ending because his division chief brought the case to a head.

Another time, an employee was causing so many problems that he was literally paralyzing his local organization. His conduct and the slew of complaints that he had been filing were tying the office up in knots and would have kept it in litigation for years to come. We decided to take a risky approach by reassigning him to another office in a different geographic area of the country.[15] We did this because he was having such an adverse impact on the office that it was inhibiting the efficiency of the federal government. Our actions shocked him and he made it clear that he did not want to relocate to that area. However, because we brought this problem to a head, and he realized we were serious, he quickly found another job.

Take as Strong an Action as You Can

One of my core beliefs is that the vast majority of government managers unintentionally misapply the concept of progressive discipline. Progressive discipline means taking increasingly stringent penalties each time an employee commits another work-related infraction. In most cases, the progression goes from an oral counseling to one or more written disciplinary actions (e.g., admonishment or reprimand) to a short and then a long suspension and, finally, to removal. The goal of progressive discipline is to change the employee's behavior using the least stringent action possible in order to try and retain her as a productive worker.

In my experience, many if not most government officials seem to feel that whenever an employee commits an infraction, they always have to take the least possible action recommended by their organization's table of penalties.[16] I firmly believe that this approach is a mistake. In my opinion, you should not give the same penalty to someone who has been AWOL for two weeks as you would to someone who has been AWOL for two hours. You should not give the same penalty to a person who has been mildly insubordinate in private as you would to an individual who has been overtly and aggressively insubordinate in public.

Tables of penalties are designed to ensure that people are treated fairly and equitably. However, they are also designed to provide management with a range of penalties from which to choose because every situation is different and managers need flexibility in dealing with problem employees. Do not fall into the trap of always choosing the least possible disciplinary action because, if you do, you may very well wind up in the nightmarish situation described earlier wherein the employee was constantly using legal protections to jerk you around.

Choosing the right disciplinary action is a key component of your overall strategy. When you are dealing with a true problem employee (as opposed to someone who commits a one-time aberration), you should choose a strong penalty that is above the minimum range in the table. After all, if you are dealing with someone who is clearly going to be a long-term problem, you know that a weak disciplinary action is not going to get his attention or change his behavior. Your best bet is to take a stronger action and bring the situation to a head as quickly as possible and not get mired down in a series of minor actions that will merely result in more and more litigation. If you take this approach and do not change that individual's behavior, you will undoubtedly reach the proposed removal phase quicker and without all of the drama that is typically associated with a long and drawn-out war of attrition.

I am not suggesting that you immediately propose someone's removal whenever they commit their first infraction. Rather, what I am saying is that you need to use your judgment when choosing a penalty, and that in many cases, it makes more sense to choose a strong penalty over a weak one. If you take this approach with chronically poor employees, you will be on the offense instead of defense, which for a government manager is a refreshing position to be in. (More on this in Chapter 6.)

Let me give you an example. A problem employee made some threatening remarks to one of our supervisors. While some organizations might have treated this softly and simply given the employee a reprimand or short suspension, we felt that threats have no place in the workplace and we proposed his removal. At his oral reply, he stood by his remarks and did not apologize for them. After considering both his oral and written replies, I let him know that I would probably sustain his removal and the employee decided to resign on the spot. Had we simply gone with a reprimand, who knows how many additional problems this individual would have given us before we finally took action to terminate him? We could have avoided even more headaches had we terminated this employee during probation.

Weeding Out Problem Employees during Probation

Taking action while the employee is still on probation is the easiest and simplest way to fire someone who is not a good fit for your organization. USAJobs.com, the official federal job site, states the following: "The probationary period is really the final and most important step in the examining process. It affords the supervisor an opportunity to evaluate the employee's performance and conduct on the job, and to remove the person without undue formality, if necessary."[17]

Throughout my career, whenever we hired a class of trainees, we often terminated one or more of them during probation. The people who are problem employees make themselves known early on. They do not pay attention in class, they frequently come to work late, and they give their instructor or their fellow trainees a hard time. Everybody knows who they are, as it is almost impossible to hide your true self for an entire year.

Once a probationary employee demonstrates that he is a problem, management has an obligation to document his deficiencies, put him on notice that he is not meeting expectations, and make a good faith effort to help him. Hopefully, he will turn around. However, if he does not, do not wait the entire year and then terminate him at the last possible moment as so many organizations seem to do. When it becomes clear that the employee is not going to make it, cut your losses, let him go, and allow him to get on with his life. This is the fairest and cleanest approach for everybody. After all, the longer you retain the employee once it has been established that he is not going to make it, the more you are simply throwing good money after bad and you may be giving the employee the misleading impression that he is going to pass probation.

Earlier in this chapter, I may have surprised you when I stated that you should document the deficiencies of a poor probationary employee. After all, many people feel that because a probationary employee has no appeal rights, you can terminate him with almost no documentation and for any reason. That is simply not true.

While probationary employees generally cannot appeal to third parties such as the MSPB, they can usually file an EEO complaint alleging prohibited discrimination. If such a complaint is filed with the EEOC, and the agency has no documentation in its case file, and the termination letter contains only a vague basis for the action, the agency will have a hard time being sustained.

The better approach is to issue the employee a termination letter that explains the reason(s) why he is being removed in sufficient detail so that he (and potentially a third party) clearly understands the rationale for the action. An example letter follows.

This is to advise you that effective March 15, 2009, you are being terminated during your probationary period for the following reasons:

a. Poor performance—In your position as a trainee customer contact representative, you are expected to answer questions from the public in an accurate manner at least 85 percent of the time. These performance standards became effective for you on December 15, 2008. However, from that date until March 1, 2009, your accuracy rate was only 63 percent.

b. Tardiness—You began work with the government on October 1, 2008. Since that date, you have arrived late for work on at least 12 occasions. Your starting time is 8:00 a.m. and you have a 15-minute grace period, meaning any time you arrive after 8:15 a.m., you are considered to be late. Several times you have been warned that your tardiness was unacceptable. Listed below are the dates and times you were late:

Date	Time You Reported for Work
10/3/08	8:30 a.m.
10/6	8:40 a.m.
10/9	8:25 a.m.
Etc.	Etc.

Some people might think that such a detailed letter is overkill for a termination during probation, but I certainly do not. It lets the probationer know exactly why he is being terminated, which is the right thing to do. It also contains so much detail that he is less likely to contest it (e.g., to EEOC or his local congressman) than had he only been provided with a vague letter. Furthermore, it paints a clear picture of management's rationale for its actions and it will help to positively shape the perspective of anyone reading it, such as an official from EEOC.

Finally, the file should contain written documentation that supports the reasons for termination, including performance records or witness statements. If you don't have the documentation available at the time you are prepared to take action, you need to gather it immediately by locating applicable documents (e.g., letters of counseling or records) and going to witnesses and asking them to prepare statements. Never ask them to back-date their accounts. Simply have them write down what happened to the best of their ability. Here is an example: "On or about December 13, 2008, at 2:30 p.m., in the third-floor conference room, I heard Mr. Jones tell his supervisor, Mrs. Brown, to 'go to hell.'"

If you follow the guidance in this chapter, you will successfully deal with any troublesome probationers that you may have, and you will save yourself a tremendous amount of aggravation in the years to come.

6

FIRING FOR
MISCONDUCT

IN THIS CHAPTER, I will explain how to fire an employee for misconduct, and I will walk you through the different steps in the process that you need to follow in order to succeed. As in other chapters of the book, the approach described herein is primarily from the perspective of the federal government, simply because of it sheer size and reach. Moreover, it would be almost impossible to explain the steps required for each state and local government entity because many of them have systems that, while similar to the federal government's, are also somewhat different. The key for managers in those organizations is to follow the principles laid out in this section (Section 2), but then to customize them to your own unique statutes, rules, and regulations.

For the most part, any government entity would also use the same approach that is described in this chapter when it is taking a lesser action, such as a reprimand or short suspension. The only difference is that once you go for a removal, the employee generally has a few more rights (e.g., a longer right to reply or more appeal rights) and the stakes are higher.

The Investigation

When an act of misconduct is brought to management's attention, the first thing management needs to do is gather the facts. This normally entails conducting an informal investigation[1] and trying to answer the following questions: (1) What happened? (2) Who did what? (3) Did what happened constitute misconduct? (4) When did it happen? (5) Where did it happen? (6) Were there mitigating circumstances?

The first-line supervisor of the person who allegedly committed the offense usually conducts the investigation, although that is not a legal requirement. Other people, such as a human resources management (HRM) specialist, could be either charged with conducting the investigation or asked to help out.

When interviewing witnesses in unionized environments, management needs to be aware that an employee is entitled to what is known as his "Weingarten right." That is, he may have union representation if a representative of the agency conducts the examination, the employee reasonably believes that the examination may result in disciplinary action, and the employee asks for representation.[2] Normally, the employee has to request representation but some union contracts require management to notify employees of that right. Make sure that you are aware of the way the Weingarten right works in your organization.

On June 15, 2004, the National Labor Relations Board (NLRB) ruled that employees who work in a nonunionized workplace are not entitled to have a coworker accompany them to an interview with their employer even if the affected employee reasonably believes that the interview might result in discipline.[3] This decision reversed the July 2000 decision of the NLRB that extended Weingarten rights to nonunion employees.[4]

As you conduct your investigation and determine who has information relevant to the alleged offense, first question each individual who may have some information regarding the incident(s) and find out what they know. This will give you a good initial sense about what just happened. Then instruct each witness to provide you with a signed and dated written statement so you will have the documentation you need in the event that you decide to take a disciplinary or adverse action.[5]

Note that sometimes witnesses are reluctant to provide statements to management because they may not want to get involved, testify against a fellow employee, or anger the union. That having been said, as employees of your organization, they are required to provide honest testimony in the event that management instructs them to do so. If they refuse, you can take a disciplinary or adverse action against them, up to and including removal for failing to cooperate in an official investigation.

I did this once when a witness refused to tell me who it was that allegedly saw one of our employees steal government supplies. I advised her that if she didn't divulge the name of that person, I would propose her removal. Reluctantly, the next day she provided me with the name, which enabled me to successfully conclude my investigation and take appropriate action.

Be aware, however, that if you take this approach you may sometimes get what you want but nothing else. In other words, if you threaten to take action, unless the employee gives you a statement(s), she may give you a statement wherein she says that she did not recall seeing anything that was inappropriate. At that point, you would then have to decide where to take this issue.

What you don't want to do is take such a heavy-handed approach against your witnesses that you create a new set of problems. After all, if all you get is a very reluctant witness providing a statement, odds are she will not make a particularly good witness in the event that she needs to testify before a third party.

One of the most common mistakes that management makes at this stage is to not speak to the employee whose conduct is in question. Many people seem to think that they should first gather the facts and propose an action, and then give the employee the opportunity to reply. The problem with this approach is that you move forward in the process without speaking to the most important person—the one against whom you may wind up taking action.

When you do this, you are setting an action in motion even though you don't have all of the facts; that could have a devastating effect on an employee. For example, imagine if you proposed someone's removal for sleeping on duty and then found out that he was a service-connected disabled veteran who was taking a new medication for the condition that made him sleepy. Under this scenario, you would probably take a different approach than trying to fire him. However, if you didn't speak to the employee and hear his side, you will most likely have wasted a lot of time and effort and created some hard feelings for nothing.

When questioning witnesses, ask them to prepare statements that describe what they saw in as much detail as possible and to date their statements. Advise them to address as many of the questions that I described earlier: Who? What? Where? When? How? and Why? However, never tell them what to write down. The statements should always be theirs, not yours, and you should never lead your witnesses.

Ask them to be as specific as possible about what they saw and heard. If the incident involved the use of inappropriate language, the following description would be inadequate, as it would be too vague: "I heard Mr. Brown curse at Mrs. Smith."

After all, if this served as the charge, the employee could argue that he is not in a position to defend himself because the statement does not indicate what he actually said.

A much better statement would be the following: "I heard Mr. Brown tell Mrs. Smith that she was 'a fat, stupid, and ignorant old fart who had no business managing a government office.'"

A statement with this degree of detail provides a much more accurate picture of what the employee said and why it was wrong. Moreover, it is fairer to the employee because it lets him know exactly what he is being charged with having said so he can defend himself in the best possible manner.

Once you have gathered the facts and decided that you will probably take some action, you should put the documents in a file. Your best bet would be to put them in date order, with the most current document placed on top. This way, it will be easy for anyone reviewing the file to follow the chain of events sequentially from the bottom to the top.

If, however, certain documents should be grouped together (i.e., copies of timecards or financial records), then you might want to organize the file into sections. If you take this approach, place dividers in the file and label them accordingly.

You should also make copies of all past counseling, disciplinary, and adverse actions that are still current, and place them in the file. By "still current," I mean that if you gave someone an admonishment that was subsequently removed from his personnel folder due to the lapse of time, it would be unfair to hold that admonishment against the employee.

The reason why you want to include these documents in the file is that it will help establish the person's pattern of behavior. This will be important down the road when determining the appropriate penalty for his offense.

The goal is to put together a file in a clear and logical manner so that anyone reading it will be able to follow the chain of events and understand the rationale for the action being taken. You would be surprised how many adverse action files I have seen—files that were poorly prepared, sloppy, and lacked some of the most basic evidence.

Anyone reviewing a file put together in this manner will get the impression that management either does not have a good case or was not willing to take the time to construct their case in a clear and convincing manner. Remember, if a case is appealed, the party that paints the most convincing picture of its position is the one that normally prevails.

As your case goes forward, continue to add other key documents to the file, such as the proposed action, a copy of the employee's written reply (including any additional evidence that she submits), a summary of her oral reply, or the decision letter. Continue to follow the same format that I described earlier so that the file is clean and professional.

Deciding What to Do

Now is the time to take a critical look at the facts in the case and determine what to do. If it looks like a strong action is going to be required, then an official who is usually above the level of the first-line supervisor must first propose the action contemplated.[6] Your organization's internal personnel manual will tell you who the proposing official is, but it typically is someone at the division or section chief level.

In deciding what to do, that individual should review the file and then, at a minimum, consult with the first-line supervisor and an HRM advisor. She should speak to the first-line supervisor in order to develop a deeper understanding of the employee whom action is contemplated against (e.g., what has been his work history, or how has he comported himself). She should consult with an HRM advisor in order to ensure that she understands the governing civil service rules and regulations; the applicable union contract issues, if any; the organization's personnel practices; and key case law.

Although it is appropriate to inform the deciding official about the action being contemplated, I strongly suggest that contact between the proposing official and the decider be kept to a bare minimum on this particular issue. Otherwise, if it later comes out that the deciding official played a role in the decision to propose the action, his independence as the deciding official will come into question and the case could easily be reversed for failure to afford the employee due process.

If the proposing official has any questions about the case, this would be a good time to either speak to one or more of the witnesses or request more documentation. If the employee is relatively new to his unit, it would also be a good idea for the proposing official to speak to one or more of his previous supervisors. In this way, the official will get a good sense of the employee's work history and a better feel for the type of employee he has been to date.

Burden of Proof

When deciding the action to propose, analyze the case as if it were about to go to a third party, such as the U.S. Merit Systems Protection Board (MSPB).[7] I suggest that you take this approach because it will provide some rigor and discipline to the decision-making process. Keep in mind that you are not legally required to do what I am recommending at this point, especially if the action you wind up taking does not meet the definition of an adverse action. This is because if the official charged with determining what to do decides to take only a disciplinary action, it will not fall within the purview of the MSPB.

On the other hand, even if she decides to propose an adverse action and finds that the case falls short of meeting the appropriate third party's "burden of proof," she may still want to go forward. That is because, as I discussed earlier, there are times when it is best to bring a case to a head and allow the deciding official to resolve the case from a position of relative strength.

By taking such an approach, all of the key players will have a good feel for the strengths and weaknesses of the case. This will ensure that the organization ultimately makes the best and most informed decision, that the organization will have a good sense as to how the case would do on appeal, and that it will have the greatest degree of flexibility possible. Moreover, if the case ultimately goes to a third party, it will have been constructed from the beginning in a format that places the agency's position in the best possible light.

If an appeal is filed with the MSPB, "The agency has the burden of proving that it was justified in taking the action. If the agency meets its burden of proof, the Board <u>must decide in favor of the agency</u>, unless (the appellant) show(s) that there was 'harmful error' in the agency's procedures, that the agency decision was based on a prohibited personnel practice, or that the decision was not in accordance with the law."[8]

In essence, the agency has to prove three elements to meet its burden: (1) It must prove its charge(s) by a preponderance of the evidence, (2) it must establish a nexus between the action taken and the efficiency of the service, and (3) it must show that the penalty selected was reasonable. In my view, if the proposing official uses this three-part test as a guide when deciding what to do, while also factoring in some of the real-world considerations that I mentioned earlier (e.g., taking a strong action against a chronically poor employee, or bringing a problem case to a head), he will definitely ensure that agency puts together the best possible proposal. Let's examine each of the three agency burdens in more detail.

With respect to proving charges, I provided the official MSPB definition of a "preponderance of the evidence" in Chapter 5 so I will not repeat that definition here. A more detailed description came from the board when it said, "[P]reponderance of the evidence exists when such evidence has, when considered and compared with that opposed to it, more convincing force and produces in the mind of the trier of fact a belief that such evidence is more likely true than not true."[9]

Still another way to think about that standard is that the agency must prove by 51 percent of the evidence presented that the employee committed the inappropriate act(s) alleged in the charges in order to prevail.

One of the challenges that the proposing official may have in determining whether a preponderance of the evidence exists is when there is a "he said, she said" situation. In this scenario, there may be only two witnesses and they each could tell a story that is diametrically opposed to the other's. What should the official do? Some people have decided that because one witness says that an employee did something wrong, while the employee denies that account, there is not a preponderance of evidence to sustain the action. I would strongly disagree with this simplistic analysis.

What the proposing official needs to do is assess the credibility of each witness and decide if either one is more credible than the other. For example, if one witness has inconsistencies in her statement, that would make her appear less credible than someone whose statement was consistent throughout. If a witness has no self-interest at stake when writing a statement, that statement is often given more weight than a statement from someone who is trying to save his skin. Should a witness appear to be less than upfront with her testimony (i.e., it looks as if she is hiding something), that would make me question the veracity of her statement. Finally, I would give more weight to a person whose statement is very detailed and specific than I would to someone whose statement is vague and inconclusive.

In assessing credibility, I would also look at other factors, such as a person's work history, relationship with the key players, possible hidden agendas, or confidence regarding their recollection of the event. Reviewing evidence is not an exact science and it requires a lot of skill and judgment, which is one reason why you also want to rely on other people to help you make your decision—additional perspectives will help you make the best decision possible.

Regarding the nexus between the action taken and the efficiency of the service, the MSPB says that this "requirement, for purposes of whether an agency has shown that its action promotes the efficiency of service, means that there must be a clear and direct relationship between the articulated grounds for an adverse action and either the employee's ability to accomplish his duties satisfactorily or some other legitimate government interest."[10]

For some cases, the nexus is rather obvious, such as in situations where the employee is AWOL. The MSPB "has long held that unauthorized absence, by its very nature, disrupts the efficiency of the service."[11] The same principal usually applies to insubordination, threatening behavior while on the job, sleeping on duty, and theft of government funds.

However, there are situations where the nexus is not as clear, especially when it involves employee behavior away from work. For instance, in *Bonnet v. The United States Postal Service*,[12] the court overturned an MSPB decision to sustain the removal of a postal manager who was indicted for, but never convicted of, indecency with a child. The board had affirmed the removal, finding that the sexual misconduct was proved and was in violation of the code of ethical conduct. The court, however, reversed the decision, finding that there was no nexus between the employee's off-duty conduct and his job performance.

In the event that the nexus is less than clear, your best bet would be to have either your HRM advisor or a government attorney research the case law. After all, there is no need to reinvent the wheel, especially because there are probably cases that have already been decided that deal with nexus issues that are similar to yours.

The good news here is that this is the easiest of the three required burdens to meet in order to prove your case, especially if it involves on-the-job conduct. If you pay attention to the factors described in this section and do your homework, you should be fine.

The third burden that management needs to meet in order to be sustained by the MSPB is that the chosen penalty must be within the bounds of reasonableness. These are commonly referred to as the "Douglas factors," which were listed in *Douglas v. Veterans Administration*.[13]

The agency is to consider these when determining the employee's penalty. On appeal, the MSPB then evaluates the penalty in light of these same factors, in an attempt to ensure that the penalty is within tolerable limits of reasonableness.

The MSPB judges are supposed to only modify the agency's penalty if a review of the factors indicates that the penalty was clearly inappropriate.

The twelve key Douglas factors are the following:

1. The employee's past work record, including length of service, performance on the job, ability to get along with fellow workers, and dependability

2. The effect of the offense upon the employee's ability to perform at a satisfactory level and its effect upon supervisors' confidence in the employee's ability to perform assigned duties

3. Consistency of the penalty with those imposed upon other employees for the same or similar offenses

4. Consistency of the penalty with any applicable agency table of penalties

5. The notoriety of the offense or its impact upon the reputation of the agency

6. The clarity with which the employee was on notice of any rules that were violated in committing the offense, or had been warned about the conduct in question

7. Potential for the employee's rehabilitation

8. The notoriety of the offense or its impact upon the reputation of the agency

9. The clarity with which the employee was on notice of any rules that were violated in committing the offense, or had been warned about the conduct in question

10. Mitigating circumstances surrounding the offense such as unusual job tensions, personality problems, mental impairment, harassment, or bad faith, malice or provocation on the part of others involved in the matter

11. The adequacy and effectiveness of alternative sanctions to deter such conduct in the future by the employee or others.[14]

If the proposing official uses these factors as a guide in deciding what to propose, he will at least be following the same basic thought process as a potential third party and be in a good position to explain his rationale. Moreover, the factors are logical and easy to apply and will help ensure that employees are treated fairly and equitably and consistent with agency policy. Let's look at several of these factors in more detail.

1. The employee's past work record, including length of service, performance on the job, ability to get along with fellow workers, and dependability.

Comment: Clearly, you would want to treat someone who has been a problem employee more severely than you would someone who has a one-time aberration on his record. Moreover, you would probably want to send a different message to a long-time dedicated employee than you would to an employee who just came on board and is already giving you problems.

2. The effect of the offense upon the employee's ability to perform at a satisfactory level and its effect upon supervisors' confidence in the employee's ability to perform assigned duties.

Comment: Some offenses (e.g., a short bout of AWOL) do not have much of an impact on the employee's ability to perform or the supervisor's confidence in him. However, misconduct such as insubordination can easily undermine the entire work unit and the employee's relationship with his supervisor, and it should be dealt with in a harsher manner.

3. Consistency of the penalty with those imposed upon other employees for the same or similar offenses.

Comment: This is simply a matter of fairness; people should be treated fairly relative to each other. That having been said, do not misunderstand this factor. Someone who is AWOL for two hours should be treated differently than someone who has been AWOL for two weeks. Someone who has a past history of misconduct and commits the same offense as someone who has no such history of misconduct should be treated differently.

4. Consistency of the penalty with any applicable agency table of penalties.

Comment: Most government agencies have a table of penalties. Whenever an act of misconduct occurs and you determine that action needs to be taken, you should turn to your agency's table. It will give you the recommended range of penalties for certain infractions (it cannot possibly cover all acts of misconduct) and will help you make a sound and justifiable decision. Managers should avoid force-fitting an offense or charge into an existing category. Rather, they should use the table as a guide for selecting a charge and penalty that fits a particular situation.

All of these factors will not apply in every case, and in many cases, some of the relevant factors will weigh in the employee's favor while others may not. Selection of the appropriate penalty must therefore involve a careful balancing of the appropriate factors in each case.

With this in mind, do not forget my earlier comments about trying to bring problem cases to a head as quickly as possible. Remember, the ultimate goal is to either change the employee or *change the employee* . . . and to do it as quickly as possible. Listed here is a portion of the U.S. Department of the Interior's Table of Penalties.

Table 6-1. U.S. Department of the Interior's (DOI) Table of Penalties.[15]

NATURE OF OFFENSE	FIRST OFFENSE	SUBSEQUENT OFFENSES	POSSIBLE CHARGES
1. An unauthorized absence from duty resulting in AWOL; excessive tardiness; leaving work before the end of duty; taking excessively long coffee or lunch breaks	Written reprimand to five-day suspension	Written reprimand to removal	Unauthorized absence from duty; tardiness; AWOL; excessive tardiness; failure to work a full tour of duty
2. Misuse of leave; failure to adhere to leave usage requirements; failing to request leave in accordance with regulations; failing to provide administratively acceptable medical certification to justify sick leave requests; excessive unscheduled medical absences	Written reprimand to five-day suspension	Written reprimand to removal	Misuse of leave; failure to adhere to proper procedures when requesting leave; unsatisfactory attendance; failure to supply proper certification
3. Unprofessional or discourteous conduct toward supervisors, co-workers or the public; use of foul language; angry outbursts; disrespectful comments; provoking quarrels; inappropriate remarks; use of abusive language or offensive language; quarreling or inciting to quarrel	Written reprimand to five-day suspension	Five-day suspension to removal	Discourteous conduct; disrespectful conduct; disruptive conduct; use of foul (also vulgar, obscene, profane or abusive) language; abusive conduct
4. Insubordination, refusal to comply with proper orders, or disregard of directives or regulations; refusing to do assigned work; failure to do assigned work; carelessness in performing assigned work	Written reprimand to 14-day suspension	5-day suspension to removal	Unprofessional or disrespectful conduct toward a supervisor; failure to follow a supervisor's instructions; failure or refusal to perform assigned duties as directed; failure to meet set deadlines

NATURE OF OFFENSE	FIRST OFFENSE	SUBSEQUENT OFFENSES	POSSIBLE CHARGES
5. Physical fighting, threatening bodily harm to another, or physical resistance to responsible authority; creating a disturbance	Written reprimand to removal	Fve-day suspension to removal	Creating a disturbance; engaging in disruptive conduct; engaging in abusive conduct; striking a co-worker; striking a supervisor; pushing another individual
6. Reporting for duty or being on duty while under the influence of alcohol or drugs; inappropriate consumption of alcohol while on duty	Written reprimand to removal	Fourteen-day suspension to removal	Drinking alcoholic beverages while on duty; performing while under the influence of intoxicants or drugs; on duty while under the influence of intoxicants or drugs
7. Sale or transfer of controlled substances on government premises or during duty hours	Five-day suspension to removal	Thirty-day suspension to removal	Unauthorized use or possession of a controlled substance on government premises; transferring or selling controlled substances on government property

Notice that there is a wide range of potential penalties that may be imposed for first and subsequent offenses. Moreover, management officials may either exceed a recommended action or take a lower one if circumstances dictate. The U.S. Department of the Interior's (DOI) written guidance, which accompanies Table 6-1, makes that clear:

> This Table does not replace supervisory judgment, as certain circumstances may warrant lesser or more severe penalties, and does not require specific penalties (for other than willful misuse of a government vehicle). . . . However, it is important to note that the supervisor retains full authority to set penalties as he/she deems appropriate based on the particular circumstances and specifications of the offense.[16]

The point is that government managers usually have more discretion than they think they have to take an action against an employee. As you can see from the table, all of the infractions carry maximum penalties for a first offense that are pretty strong (i.e., suspension or removal). Moreover, if the first offense were severe enough (e.g., a long bout of AWOL without mitigating circumstances), I would strongly consider exceeding the table when proposing a penalty.

Regardless of the penalty that you choose, you should always have a solid rationale for your decision that is grounded in the Douglas factors. If you do and you can clearly explain why you chose the penalty that you did, odds are that you will eventually prevail.

Now that we've discussed a government agency's typical burden of proof, let's get back to deciding what to do. As you examine the evidence, the first thing you need to decide is whether the person did something wrong. If you conclude that they did, you need to be clear about exactly what the person did that was wrong. This may sound simple, and sometimes it is, but other times this can be quite tricky.

For example, a relatively simple case usually involves AWOL. If the person was absent from work, the absence was not officially approved (i.e., leave was not granted), and the employee's timecard was clearly marked as AWOL, that should result in a relatively straightforward charge. However, let's say that the same employee did not come to work for three days, did not call his supervisor during that same period of time, had plenty of sick leave in his account, and brought a doctor's note when he returned stating that he was incapacitated during those three days. Under these circumstances, instead of charging him AWOL, the better charge would be failure to follow proper leave procedures.

I say this because employees are legally entitled to use sick leave when they are incapacitated, as this example employee was. According to *Valenzuela v. Department of the Army*, December 21, 2007,[17]

> . . . a charge of AWOL will not be sustained if the appellant presents administratively acceptable evidence that he was incapacitated for duty during the relevant period if the employee has sufficient sick leave to cover the period of absence. Grubb v. Department of the Interior, 96 M.S.P.R. 377, ¶ 36 (2004); Wesley, 94 M.S.P.R. 277, ¶ 18. Agencies may take disciplinary action against an employee based on his failure to follow leave-requesting procedures and his use of unscheduled leave provided he is clearly on notice of such requirements and the likelihood of discipline for continued failure to comply. Allen v. U.S. Postal Service, 88 M.S.P.R. 491, ¶ 10 (2001).

You may be asking yourself, "How am I supposed to know all of this stuff? I am not an expert in HRM so how can I possibly avoid some of the pitfalls that will surely come my way?" The answer is that you cannot become an HRM expert overnight, any more than I can expect to become a nurse, a physicist, a statistician, or a claims processor without years of training. However, by the time you finish reading this book, you will know enough to at least ask the right questions and you will understand the key philosophies, strategies, and tactics to apply in order to remove a poor government employee. If you surround yourself with strong advisors and learn to follow your agency's rules and regulations and, where applicable, the union contract, you will succeed the vast majority of time.

Once you are clear about what the person did wrong, you should list the individual offense(s) on a piece of paper. These are not the formal charges yet, simply a frame of reference for moving forward.

You then should determine if a preponderance of the evidence supports each charge. Review all of the witness statements and other documentary evidence to make sure that, on balance, they are consistent with the offense(s) that you believe the employee committed.

Note that you are not a trier of fact at this point; you would only be the proposing official, so you do not need to have a legally perfect case. On several occasions, weak proposed removals came to me, as the deciding official, which I knew would not be sustained by a third party. Sometimes I found for the employee. However, on most occasions, it was clear to everyone (i.e., the supervisors, the employee, the union, and me) that the employee was a problem so we used the proposed removal as a mechanism to negotiate a settlement that was in everybody's best interest. These settlements generally ranged from a resignation to an application for disability retirement to a last-chance agreement (more on that later). The point is that you do not always need to propose a legally strong case in order to effectively deal with a problem employee.

That having been said, the better your case, the better your chance of ultimately prevailing, and so always try and do the best you can to meet the burden of proof I referenced earlier.

Your next step is to ensure that there is a nexus that will show how the action you are about to propose will promote the efficiency of the government. Again, as long as the proposal does not relate to off-duty conduct, this should be relatively easy to demonstrate. However, you must make sure to explicitly state what the nexus is in the proposed action, the supporting documents, or both. Otherwise, down the road, you may have to hope that the ultimate adjudicator of the case will see the nexus without formally hearing or reading about your rationale.

Regarding the penalty, look at your table of penalties and apply all of the Douglas factors. Recognize that you have a lot of flexibility in choosing the appropriate penalty, so use that flexibility wisely. Keep in mind the following rules of thumb because they address the issues of progressive discipline and both multiple and dissimilar offenses:

> ➤ Offenses need not be identical in order to support progressively more severe disciplinary/adverse action against an employee. For example, an employee who has received an admonishment for AWOL can receive a reprimand for sleeping on duty, and possibly be suspended or removed for a third offense unrelated to the two previous infractions.

> ➤ When an employee has committed a combination or series of offenses, a greater penalty than listed for a single offense is appropriate.[18]

> ➤ Supervisors are normally held to a higher standard of conduct than non-supervisors. That is "because they occupy positions of trust and responsibility."[19]

On rare occasions, agencies may not have much discretion in setting penalties. For example, Title 31 of the United States Code (U.S.C.), Section 1344(a):

> prohibits the use of a U.S. Government-owned or -leased vehicle for other than official purposes. The law also states that any officer or employee who willfully uses or authorizes the use of a U.S. Government vehicle for other than official purposes will be suspended for at least one month without pay by the head of the agency (31 U.S.C. 1349(b)).[20]

If you are dealing with this situation, you may legally take an even stronger action but not a weaker one.

With all of the information at hand, the proposing official should look carefully at the facts; refer to the controlling rules, regulations, and case law; and make a tentative decision. He then should run his findings by his key advisors, who should provide him with some objective and technically sound advice. Once the final decision has been made to propose an action (for the sake of this discussion, we'll assume it is a proposed removal), it is time to write the proposal letter.

Writing and Issuing the Proposed Removal

The letter itself is pretty standard, in the sense that it should contain all of the requisite information (i.e., who to respond to and where to get copies of the applicable records), timeframes (i.e., when the oral and/or written replies are due and, in the event that a decision is made to remove the employee, the earliest date that the removal will occur). Later on in this chapter, I will provide you with a sample proposed removal letter.

The most important part of writing the proposal, as well as the trickiest, is writing the charges. On the surface, this seems like it would be a rather simple thing to do. But as we shall see, it requires a reasonable amount of skill and expertise. Moreover, if a removal goes to a third party, that party will adjudicate the case and determine whether the agency met its burden of proof *relative to the way the charges were written* and not relative to what the employee allegedly did or did not do. Accordingly, understanding the proper way to write a charge is absolutely crucial to prevailing before a third party.

To start, according to the United States Court of Appeal for the Federal Circuit, "[W]hen an agency proposes to discipline an employee, it must notify the employee of the conduct with which he is charged 'in sufficient detail to permit the employee to make an informed reply."[21] Agencies typically fulfill their responsibility to give notice by designating a particular charge and accompanying the charge with a narrative description setting forth the details of the charged misconduct."[22] The narrative description, which is also referred to as the specification, contains the factual basis for each charge.

In order to provide the employee with sufficient detail, make sure that the charge describes the who, what, when, and where of the misconduct. Be as specific as you can about the employee's actions. For example, do not simply say "you acted inappropriately toward your supervisor" but describe the actual actions that were inappropriate.

By the same token, do not place so much information in the charge that it clouds the issue and makes it unclear what you are actually charging the employee with. If you place too much information in the charge, you may increase your burden of proof because you may be required to prove these issues even though they are, at best, tangential to the actual charge.

In writing the charge, the proposing official should make sure that the facts fit the charge. In other words, make sure that the charge represents the employee's actual misconduct. In addition, do not overcharge the employee. In *Acox v. USPS*, 76 M.S.P.R. 111, 113 (1997), the employee was charged with "verbal abuse and physical threats made to another employee." The MSPB ultimately decided that the agency could not split its charge based on a single act. The board further determined that the agency had to prove that the employee's misconduct constituted both verbal abuse and physical threats. Ultimately, the MSPB found against the agency but indicated that, had the agency labeled the charge as only "verbal abuse of another employee," it would have sustained the charge.

You also must be careful about how you label a charge because that could have a major impact on your burden of proof. For example, the MSPB treats a charge of insubordination differently than it does a failure to follow instructions charge. Insubordination consists of a "willful and intentional refusal to obey an authorized order of a superior, which the superior is entitled to have obeyed."[23] It is the more difficult of the two charges to prove because management would have to demonstrate that a clear order or instruction was given, that an individual with the proper authority issued it, that it was within the ability of the recipient to comply, and that it was disobeyed. Unlike insubordination, a charge of "failure to follow instructions" does not require proof that the failure was intentional.[24] The agency would only have to show that proper instructions were given to the employee and that the employee did not follow those instructions.

Try not to charge the employee with violating a law, rule, or regulation because that greatly increases your burden of proof. If you merely charge an employee with some form of inappropriate behavior, you only have to prove the misconduct; whereas if you charge the employee with violating a statute, you have to prove the misconduct and show how the statute was violated, which is a much more difficult burden.

For example, if an employee sexually harasses a coworker, the charge in the proposal notice may read "Sexual harassment in violation of 29 C.F.R. § 1604.11(a)." To prevail in this charge, an agency would have to prove that (1) sexual harassment occurred and (2) 29 C.F.R. § 1604.11(a), an EEOC regulation on sexual harassment, was violated. However, if the agency simply charges the employee with "inappropriate conduct of a sexual nature," the agency will only have to prove that the employee engaged in misconduct that was sexual in nature.[25]

Finally, if you charge the employee with multiple instances of misconduct, be aware of the ramifications of that decision. For example, if you prevail only on some but not all of the charges, this could have an impact on the ultimate penalty. The MSPB states, "Where the agency proves fewer than all of its charges, the Board may not independently determine a reasonable penalty. Rather, the Board may mitigate to the maximum reasonable penalty so long as the agency has not indicated, either in its final decision or during proceedings before the Board, that it desires that a lesser penalty be imposed on fewer charges."[26]

Let's take a look at a few possible charges.

"On December 15, 2007, you yelled at your coworker, Ms. Jeannette Jones. Your behavior was unacceptable."

Analysis: This charge is too vague. It does not mention the time or the location where the employee is alleged to have committed the offense. Moreover, it does not indicate what he actually said to her. Last, the statement that his "behavior was unacceptable" is too broad. Ms. Brown would have a good argument that she did not have enough information in which to defend herself.

The following would be a better charge:

"At 10:30 a.m. on December 15, in room 12B, you spoke to Ms. Jeanette Jones in an inappropriate manner. Specifically, you called her a 'bitch' and a 'whore' in front of several employees. Your use of offensive language is unacceptable."

Another way to frame that same charge would be as follows:

Charge: Using offensive language

Specification: "At 10:30 am on December 15, in room 12B, you spoke to Ms. Jeanette Jones in an inappropriate manner. Specifically, you called her a 'bitch' and a 'whore' in front of several employees."

Both examples contain a charge and a specification and enough information that the employee clearly knows what he allegedly did wrong.

Below is a different charge that has some problems:

"On May 28, 2008, you were absent without authorization for three hours. Such conduct is unacceptable."

Analysis: The charge is unclear about which hours the employee was absent. Moreover, the agency is charging the employee with "unauthorized absence" instead of AWOL, which is the stronger charge.

A better way to write this would be the following:

"On May 28, 2008, from 8:00 a.m. to 11:00 a.m., you were absent from duty without permission and were charged absent without official leave (AWOL) for three hours."

Another way to frame the same charge follows:

Charge: Absence without official leave (AWOL)

Specification: "On May 28, 2008, from 8:00 a.m. to 11:00 a.m., you were absent from duty without permission and were charged AWOL for three hours."

There are a couple of other things to consider prior to issuing the letter. According to the code of federal regulations:

> If the agency determines that the employee's continued pres-
> ence in the workplace during the notice period may pose a
> threat to the employee or others, result in loss of or damage
> to Government property, or otherwise jeopardize legitimate
> Government interests, the agency may elect one or a combi-
> nation of the following alternatives: (i) Assigning the employ-
> ee to duties where he or she is no longer a threat to safety,
> the agency mission, or to Government property; (ii) Allowing
> the employee to take leave, or carrying him or her in an
> appropriate leave status (annual, sick, leave without pay, or
> absence without leave) if the employee has absented himself
> or herself from the worksite without requesting leave,[27] [or]
> placing the employee in a paid, non-duty status for such time
> as is necessary to effect the action.[28]

You should strongly consider this approach when the alleged offense(s) is considered to be particularly severe (e.g., fighting, threatening another employee, falsifying records). Moreover, bear in mind that if you do not take one or more of the above actions during the notice period, the employee may argue that if he were allowed to continue as normal pending the final decision, how serious could the offense have really been?

Also, in the event that the agency has "reasonable cause to believe that the employee committed a crime for which a sentence of imprisonment may be imposed,"[29] the agency may invoke the "crime provision," which enables it to curtail the notice period to as little as seven days. The agency may invoke this provision even if there has been no judicial action to date.

Sample Proposed Removal Letter

The following proposed removal sample letter contains a series of notes and additional information (*they are in italics*).

(Name of Employee)

(Organization Element)

(City, State, and Zip Code)

Subject: Proposed Removal

1. I propose to remove you from employment with (*name of agency*) based on the following reasons:

    A. At 10:30 a.m. on December 15, in room 12B, you spoke to Ms. Jeanette Jones in an inappropriate manner. Specifically, you called her a "bitch" and a "whore" in front of several employees. Your use of offensive language is unacceptable.

    B. On May 28, 2008, from 8:00 a.m. to 11:00 a.m., you were absent from duty without permission and were charged absent without official leave (AWOL) for three hours.

2. You have the right to reply to this notice orally, or in writing, or both orally and in writing, and to submit affidavits in support of your reply showing why this notice is inaccurate and any other reasons why your removal should not be effected. The evidence on which this notice of proposed action is based will be available for your review in the Human Resources Office, (*Room _____*). You will be allowed eight (*you could give more*) hours of official duty time for reviewing the evidence relied on to support the reason(s) in this notice, preparing your written reply, gathering affidavits in support of your case, and making a personal reply. Arrangements for the use of official time or requests for additional time should be made with me. You have the right to be represented in this matter (*e.g., a union official or an attorney*).

3. You will be given until the close of business (*date*) to reply to these reasons orally or in writing, or

both orally and in writing. (*The employee is usually given 7 to 14 calendar days to respond, depending in part on whether he is covered by a negotiated agreement.*) Your written reply should be submitted to (*deciding official*). He will receive your oral reply or will designate an official or officials to receive it.

4. If you do not understand the above reason(s) why I am proposing your removal, contact me or (*name*), of the Human Resources Management Office (*provide location and phone numbers of each*) for further explanation.

5. On two previous occasions you committed infractions and were disciplined accordingly. On the first occasion, you were charged AWOL for 16 hours and received a reprimand dated (*insert date*). On the second occasion, you were suspended in a letter dated (*insert date*) for 14 days due to your use of inappropriate language and for failure to follow proper procedures. This past record will be taken into account in determining proper disciplinary action, if one or more of the above reasons are sustained. You may reply orally or in writing, or both orally and in writing, with respect to these previous infractions and penalties and you may submit supporting evidence, including affidavits. In this regard, you may make a statement expressing your views as to the consideration to be given such past record in determining proper action. (*Citing an employee's past disciplinary record is used to support the penalty chosen. It is not the basis for the current action. It can be used if the employee was aware of the action(s), the employee had the chance to contest it, it is still timely (e.g., has not been withdrawn), and it was a matter of record. Copies of the past record must be included in the evidence file.*

I have seen certain organizations also list previous oral and written counselings here. I would not do so because they are not considered to be disciplinary actions. I recommend including them in the file and referring to them in the Douglas factors' statement, which I will address later on in this section.

Some organizations also recommend that the proposing official address each of the Douglas factors, either

*in the proposal letter or in a supplemental statement
that goes in the file. To me, this is overkill, especially because sometimes when you write too much, it
can come back to haunt you. For example, if the proposing official and the deciding official give different reasons for their penalty selection, a third
party may use that against them. In my opinion, the
proposing official should simply consider the Douglas
factors and the deciding official should add a supplemental statement to the file that addresses the
Douglas factors and gives his rationale for the
penalty he selected.*

*The reason why an agency would want to address the
Douglas factors in writing is to document its justi-
fication for the decision and make it easier for a
third party to find for it.)*

5. The final decision to effect the action proposed has
   not been made. Mr(s). (*the deciding official*), who
   will make the final decision, will give full and
   impartial consideration to your replies if submitted.

6. If it is the decision of Mr(s). (*the deciding official)* that you be removed, your removal will be
   effective not fewer than 30 calendar days from the
   day after the date of receipt of this notice.

7. You will be given a written decision as soon as possible after your replies have had full consideration,
   or after the close of business on (*same date as in
   paragraph 3 above*), if you do not reply.

8. You will be retained in an active duty status during
   the advance notice period.

_____   _____

(Signature of appropriate official)   Date

"I acknowledge receipt of this document"

_____   _____

(Signature of employee)   Date

Once the proposed removal has been prepared, the proposing official should call into his office the employee and give him the notice. This is usually a very emotional meeting and you do not want to embarrass the employee in front of his coworkers. You might even want to have some tissues handy because employees often become teary-eyed when they receive a proposed removal.

Although management is not required to notify employees prior to the meeting that they can have representation at the meeting (unless there is a contractual obligation), it is a good idea to tell them. First of all, I think it is the right thing to do, and you want to stay consistent with your core values, even if you are dealing with a poor employee. Second, the representative will generally play a relatively constructive role at this meeting (although that may change later) and try and keep the employee calm and to clarify the issues at hand.

I would also recommend that an HRM specialist be present to answer any technical questions regarding procedure, access to evidence, or other matters. Also, from the proposing official's perspective, it is always a good idea to have another management official present in awkward situations such as these because you may wind up being accused of saying or doing something inappropriate at this meeting, and it is good to have a friendly witness present.

Considering the Employee's Response

The ball is now in the employee's court, and there is nothing for the deciding official to do but wait for the employee's response. Usually what happens is the employee and his representative first request a copy of the evidence file and then begin to craft a written response. They may even request copies of certain documents that are not in the file. Such requests should be referred to HRM so that it may determine whether these items will be released.

Eventually, the employee will schedule a date and time to submit his written reply and make his oral reply. The deciding official should carefully review the written reply prior to the oral reply. This way, the official will have the opportunity to clarify any questions he has about the written reply during the formal oral reply meeting.

The official should also analyze the employee's response, which may include written evidence, in the context of the three key burdens of proof. (Does a preponderance of evidence support the charge[s]? Is there a nexus? Is removal the appropriate penalty?) More important, the official should ask himself whether removing the employee is the right thing to do. He should also discuss the employee's reply with his key HRM advisor in order to clarify any technical issues that may have been raised (e.g., reasonable accommodation or citation of applicable MSPB decisions). Finally, the deciding official should refrain from making his decision until after he has heard the employee's oral reply. After all, the written reply is only part of the employee's affirmative defense.

The oral reply meeting should be held in a private location, such as an office or conference room. I strongly recommend that the deciding official have an HRM official present at the oral reply to take notes of the meeting.[30] HRM's presence allows the deciding official to concentrate on the employee's reply and will provide him with a second set of ears in the event that his recollection of the meeting is less than crystal clear.

The deciding official should begin the meeting with some small talk in order to put the employee and his representative at ease and to keep the level of tension down. From there, he should set the stage by informing everyone about the purpose of the meeting and what to expect.

For example, the official might say, "We are here today for Mr. Smith's oral reply to his proposed removal. Ms. Jones is here as Mr. Smith's representative, and Mr. Brown from HRM is here to take notes and answer any technical questions that may arise. I would like Mr. Smith and Ms. Jones to first present the oral reply, including any evidence that you may wish to offer in support of your position. After that, I will ask a series of questions in order to clarify points that you have raised and to ensure that I understand all of the issues involved. This meeting will last as long as is necessary to ensure that you have had every opportunity to present your case as fairly and as accurately as possible."

The deciding official should try and ensure that the meeting follows this format, and that the employee and his representative stay on point to the maximum extent possible. It is also a good idea to try and determine the facts that both sides agree on and those they do not. This will allow the deciding official to narrow his focus and concentrate on clarifying the areas of disagreement. He should even review the three burdens of proof and ask the employee to comment on them, especially the Douglas factors. It is better to hear all of these arguments now rather than be surprised by them at a third-party hearing. Moreover, if you ask the employee to state his position on these issues at this time, he will be hard pressed to change his argument later on.

Once the reply has been concluded, the deciding official should make a closing statement that tells the employee and his representative what to expect. It should go something like this: "Thank you for taking the time to make your oral reply today. We will make a summary of your reply and provide a copy to you for your review. I will take my time in reviewing all of the evidence and make my decision as soon as I can. If you have any further questions, please feel free to contact either me or Mr. Brown."

At this point, the deciding official should take some time to allow the emotion of the meeting to pass so that he can review the case in a dispassionate manner. He should carefully analyze all of the evidence; review any applicable statutes, regulations, agency policies, labor agreements, and case law; the organization's table of penalties; and any other material that has been gathered for the case. He should also consult with his HRM advisor and the employee's supervisor(s) and consider discussing the matter with the person who would represent him if the case went to a third party (usually a government attorney). This way, the supervisor will have a wide variety of perspectives and get a sense about what his chances would be of prevailing on appeal should he decide to remove the employee.

If the official decides to sustain one or more of the charges but reduce the penalty, he should still consider the consequences of that decision. By this I mean, if he determines that this is a problem employee who has committed a serious offense but, for whatever reason, he concludes that removal is not appropriate (e.g., the penalty is too strong or he does not think a third party will sustain the removal), he should recognize that there is a good chance that this employee may commit another offense down the road. If that is the case, the penalty should (1) send the employee the message that continued acts of misbehavior could soon result in his removal and (2) position the agency so that it could more easily remove the employee the next time he commits a serious offense.

Obviously, whatever penalty the deciding official selects needs to be based on the facts and needs to take into account the Douglas factors.

However, that having been said, making decisions on proposed removals is more an art than a science. One way to mitigate the removal would be to give the employee a suspension of 14 days or less. The advantage of this approach is that from a progressive discipline standpoint, the next logical step would often be removal, especially if the suspension is 10 days or longer.

In most cases, I would not recommend suspending the employee for more than 14 days because that would still give the employee the right to appeal to the MSPB. If you have to try your case before the MSPB, it is better to be arguing for a removal.

Another approach you can take, which certainly has its advantages, is to have the employee sign a "last-chance agreement." Under such an agreement, the employee is given a last chance to change her behavior. In exchange for not being removed, she agrees that one more instance of misconduct within a set period of time will result in her termination and she waives her right to appeal to the MSPB. As a general rule, a waiver of appeal rights is enforceable, unless the employee can show that (1) while she complied with the agreement, the agency breached it; (2) she did not voluntarily enter into the agreement; or (3) the agreement was caused by fraud or mutual mistake.

An employee who signs a last-chance settlement agreement is entitled to receive due process.[31] This means that if you subsequently remove her for violating the last-chance agreement, according to *Licausi v. OPM*, she "must be told in what way . . . she allegedly breached the agreement. Otherwise, the appellant will not know what . . . she has to prove was not done."[32]

Assuming the supervisor decides to remove the employee, the deciding official should prepare a statement that addresses the Douglas factors he considered. This statement is extremely important and should explain why he decided that removal was the appropriate penalty. In a sense, this is his opportunity to frame the issue and make it easier for a third party to find for the government.

The Douglas factors' statement should contain a careful analysis of each factor as it applies to this particular employee; it should not contain the same language that was used to support previous removals. Otherwise, it may appear that the statement is a sham and the deciding official merely went through the motions in order to be sustained. If that happens, the agency runs a strong risk of being reversed.

The Decision Letter

What a decision letter should look like is shown below. As with the sample proposal removal letter, it contains a series of notes and additional information (*that are in italics*).

Sample Decision Letter

```
(Name of Employee)
(Organization Element)
(City, State, and Zip Code)


SUBJECT: Removal
1. In connection with the letter of (date) in which you
   were given advance notice of your proposed removal, I
   have decided to remove you from employment effective
   (date), based on the following reasons:
```

(List the sustained reasons(s)

The decision should be delivered to the employee within a reasonable period of time prior to the effective date of the removal (review your agency's human resources manual and/or your union contract to see if a specific number of days are required). In all cases, the employee must receive the decision letter on or before the date the action will be effective. Also, unless you are invoking the "crime provision," make sure that the effective date is at least 30 days from the date of the proposed removal.)

```
2. In reaching this decision, I carefully considered
   your oral and written replies (only if submitted)
   along with all of the evidence developed. My decision
   also takes into account your past disciplinary record
   as shown in your notice of proposed removal. (This
```
only applies if the deciding official considered the past record.)

```
3. I have also considered other factors, including your
   past work record, which covers your length of serv-
   ice; your performance on the job; the effect of your
   offense(s) (be clear about whether you considered one
   or more than one offense) upon your ability to per-
```

form at a satisfactory level and its effect upon your
supervisors' confidence in your ability to perform
your assigned duties; the consistency of the penalty
with those imposed upon other employees for the same
or similar offenses; the consistency of the penalty
with the agency table of penalties; the notoriety of
the offense or its impact upon the reputation of the
agency; the clarity with which you were on notice of
any rules that were violated in committing the
offense, or had been warned about the conduct in
question; your potential for rehabilitation; mitigating circumstances surrounding the offense; the adequacy and effectiveness of alternative sanctions to
deter such conduct in the future by you or others;
and your potential for rehabilitation. A more
detailed statement regarding these factors is contained in the evidence file. (*The above wording
should be modified according to both the facts of the
case and the specific factors considered.*)

I have concluded that the charges against you that
I have sustained are of such seriousness that mitigation of the proposed penalty is not appropriate, and
that the penalty of removal is reasonable and the
right thing to do.

4. You have the right to appeal this action to the
Regional Director, Merit Systems Protection Board
(MSPB), (*address*). Your appeal must be received by the
office of the MSPB no later than thirty (30) calendar
days after the effective date of this removal. The
board requires personal delivery during normal business hours by regular mail, facsimile (fax: (*telephone*)), or commercial overnight delivery service. A
copy of the board's regulations and appeal form are
attached. Petitions of appeal may be in any format,
including letter form, but must contain the information specified on the appeal form.

(*If your labor management agreement gives the employee the right to contest the removal with an arbitrator, that should be discussed here. Note that the
employee would have to decide whether to appeal the
removal to either an arbitrator or the MSPB because
he cannot appeal to both.*

If the employee raises a medical condition and

> *argues that it prevented him from doing his job, this*
> *would be a good time to notify him of his option to*
> *file a request for disability retirement with the*
> *OPM. In addition, if he alleges discrimination,*
> *inform him of his right to file a complaint with the*
> *agency's Office of Equal Employment Opportunity*
> *[EEO]. The employee may elect to file an appeal with*
> *the MSPB or to file a complaint with the EEO office,*
> *but he may not elect to file with both.)*
>
> 6. You may ask me any questions you have about this
>   removal and I will try and answer them for you. A
>   further explanation of your appeal rights may be
>   obtained by consulting the Human Resources Management
>   Office.
>
> _____   _____
> (Signature of appropriate official)   Date
>
> "I acknowledge receipt of this document"
>
> _____   _____
> (Signature of employee)   Date

You now have accomplished what many government managers have never done: fired a government employee. That is not something to celebrate because nobody likes to see a person lose his or her job. However, take comfort in knowing that you did what you believed was the right thing for the right reasons.

Also, be aware that the time shortly after the decision is given to the employee may be an appropriate time to try and find a mutually agreeable settlement. I do not mean one where the employee returns to work; that obviously is not the objective. I am referring to a settlement wherein the employee resigns or agrees to retire in exchange for a clean record and perhaps a small cash settlement. This approach accomplishes several goals: (1) The agency ensures that the employee will not return because he waives all appeal rights as part of the settlement, (2) the agency saves the cost of trying to defend its removal action on appeal, (3) the employee gets to leave with his head held high, and (4) the rest of the employees get the message that if you commit one or more acts of misconduct you will lose your job with the government.

On the other hand, I would be less likely to settle with an "employee from hell," especially if I have a strong case. After all, we all have an obligation to future employers and it would be unfair to let this employee have a clean record and allow him to approach another organization that would be unaware of his background. While this is easier said than done, and we would all like to rid ourselves of this type of employee once and for all, how would you like it if you hired another employee from hell because his last employer gave him a clean record?

Although there will be other opportunities to settle down the road (e.g., prior to a hearing), this is a particularly good time because the employee is now dealing with the shock of losing his job and worrying about how he is going to find another one, given that he has just been fired from the federal government. On the other hand, do not bend too far to settle because you need to be clear that there is a serious price to be paid for misconduct. If you handle these situations correctly, you will find that sometimes you will settle and other times you will take a stand and fight. Both results are fine if you are doing them for the right reasons.

In Chapter 8, I will talk about what happens at a third-party hearing involving a removal. Moreover, I will tell you how to prepare for such a hearing so that you are in the best possible position to win.

7

FIRING FOR POOR PERFORMANCE

IN THIS CHAPTER, I will explain how to fire a person for poor performance. As with Chapter 6, I will walk you through all of the steps that you need to follow in order to succeed. The approach continues to be from the perspective of the federal government; however, the principles described herein apply equally to state and local governments.

Overview

The goal of a performance management system is to ensure that the organization and all of its components are working together to achieve the desired outcomes. This is accomplished with the establishment of the organization's goals and metrics and then through the alignment of all the organization's management systems (e.g., structural, technical, decision-making and information, people, rewards and recognition, and renewal systems).

Goals and metrics should be established at every level of the organization, with the expectation that there will be a clear line of sight from the broad goals at the top down to the individual employee. High-performing organizations measure progress and take appropriate action toward achieving those goals at every level by (1) establishing performance expectations or standards, (2) tracking and measuring progress toward meeting those expectations, (3) providing feedback to those people whose job it is to achieve the results, (4) taking steps to improve performance where necessary, and (5) rewarding excellent performance.

Much of the above is done at the program, division, section, or team level, in recognition that the overall performance of an organization is a function of people working together as a team. However, people also have discrete jobs and organizations are often as strong as their weakest links; hence, setting standards, tracking performance, and providing feedback also must be done at the individual level because the better each employee performs, the more likely it is that the organization will achieve its goals.

Within this context, nearly every government organization sets up its own individual performance appraisal system. The objective of each system is to improve overall organizational performance by tracking how each employee performs relative to his or her standards. From my perspective, there are two key components of any performance management system: (1) the system itself and (2) the way that the system is administered. Most government organizations have reasonably sound performance management systems, although many of the standards themselves are vague and difficult to enforce. The big problem tends to be the administration of the system, particularly as it relates to poor performers.

If a government organization can get to the point where it reliably rewards excellent performance and, conversely, reliably takes action against poor performers, it will be well ahead of the game. Far too often, people are rewarded for no rhyme nor reason; by the same token, poor performers seem to skate by much more frequently than they are dealt with, which undermines the credibility of the system. A sound performance management system can only work if it is properly administered, meaning that top performers are rewarded and poor performers are dealt with fairly and firmly.

Before we begin, it is important that the reader understand the way that government performance management systems work. Once that has been accomplished, I will explore how to deal with poor performers and show you how to fire them, if necessary. This way you will be able to use the system to your best possible advantage.

Performance Appraisal System

Within the federal government, the OPM requires each agency to do the following:

> "develop one or more performance appraisal systems for employees. . . . An agency appraisal system shall establish agency-wide policies and parameters for the application and operation of performance appraisal within the agency for the employees covered by the system. At a minimum, an agency system shall–
>
> (1) Provide for–
>
>> (i)   Establishing employee performance plans, including, but not limited to, critical elements and performance standards;
>> (ii)   Communicating performance plans to employees at the beginning of an appraisal period;
>> (iii) Evaluating each employee during the appraisal period on the employee's elements and standards;
>> (iv)   Recognizing and rewarding employees whose performance so warrants;
>> (v)   Assisting employees in improving unacceptable performance; and
>> (vi)   Reassigning, reducing in grade, or removing employees who continue to have unacceptable performance, but only after an opportunity to demonstrate acceptable performance."[1]

OPM is required to review agency performance appraisal systems in order to ensure that they meet statutory and regulatory requirements.[2] Once a system is approved, the agency is free to implement it.

With respect to appraisal systems, the OPM has some key definitions that you need to be aware of as follows:

> *"Critical element* means a work assignment or responsibility of such importance that unacceptable performance on the element would result in a determination that an employee's overall performance is unacceptable.

Such elements shall be used to measure performance only at the individual level.

Non-critical element means a dimension or aspect of individual, team, or
organizational performance, exclusive of a critical element, that is used in
assigning a summary level. Such elements may include, but are not limited to, objectives, goals, program plans, work plans, and other means of
expressing expected performance.

Performance rating means the written, or otherwise recorded, appraisal of
performance compared to the performance standard(s) for each critical
and non-critical element on which there has been an opportunity to perform for the minimum period . . .

Performance standard means the management-approved expression of the
performance threshold(s), requirement(s), or expectation(s) that must be
met to be appraised at a particular level of performance. A performance
standard may include, but is not limited to, quality, quantity, timeliness,
and manner of performance.

Progress review means communicating with the employee about performance compared to the performance standards of critical and non-critical
elements."[3]

Agencies generally have two types of appraisal systems: a pass/fail system
or a multi-tiered system. Under a pass/fail system, employees can receive
only two possible ratings: pass or fail. Moreover, by definition, there are no
noncritical elements, so employees only work under critical elements. If an
employee ultimately fails one or more critical elements, she will receive a rating of "unacceptable" and is required to be removed from her position
through reassignment, demotion, or termination.[4]

I am not a big fan of this approach because it lets managers off the hook
by allowing them to avoid making meaningful distinctions between employees. It treats an outstanding employee and a marginal employee the exact
same way, which to me is counterproductive. Its only real use is for taking
action against poor employees, which is a good thing. However, it discour-
ages management from taking a more comprehensive approach toward
appraising employees and encouraging them to improve, which is a shame.

A multi-tiered system requires management to make meaningful distinctions between its employees, which is definitely a good thing. It does this

by including both critical and noncritical elements in the performance plan. Employees know where they stand relative to the organization's expectations, and management is expected then to use the appraisal as a basis for a variety of personnel actions, ranging from promotions to within-grade increases (WGI) to awards.

Multi-tiered systems can have up to five different summary levels of performance. For example, "outstanding," "excellent," "fully successful," "less than fully successful," and "unacceptable" would constitute five distinct levels. The distinctions would be based on how an employee does on both the critical and noncritical elements. Listed below is an example of how that might work:

> ➤ Outstanding: Far exceeding all critical and noncritical elements
> ➤ Excellent: Far exceeding all critical elements; at least meeting all noncritical elements
> ➤ Fully successful: At least meeting all critical and noncritical elements
> ➤ Less than fully successful: At least meeting all critical elements; failing to meet at least one noncritical element
> ➤ Unacceptable: Failing at least one critical element

Regardless of the appraisal system under which they work, employees are expected to periodically receive feedback from management about how they are doing.

Performance Standards

For all intents and purposes, managing individual employee performance begins with each employee's performance standards. Unlike a position description, which tells the employee what he is supposed to do, the performance standards advise the employee *how he is supposed to do his job.* Failure to achieve one or more of the critical elements of a job is the only way an employee may be removed for poor performance under 5 C.F.R. Part 432.

The process begins at the start of each appraisal year when the agency develops performance standards for every position (the standards are usually the same from year to year, although they may vary as legislation, technology, resources, or expectations change) and provides a copy to the employee. This is one of the most important components of the appraisal system because everyone is ultimately appraised based on how they do relative to these standards. To some extent, an agency's performance appraisal system is only as good as the way that the standards are written (and applied) because it is very difficult to hold employees accountable if they are working under poorly or imprecisely written standards.

To provide you with some insight into the way performance standards should be written, official guidance on this topic from the OPM follows:

> **General Measures.** Performance standards should be objective, measurable, realistic, and stated clearly in writing (or otherwise recorded). The standards should be written in terms of specific measurers that will be used to appraise performance. In order to develop specific measurers, you first must determine the general measure(s) that are important for each element. General measurers used to measure employee performance include the following:
>
> ➤ Quality addresses how well the work is performed and/or how accurate or how effective the final product is. Quality refers to accuracy, appearance, usefulness, or effectiveness.
>
> ➤ Quantity addresses how much work is produced . . .
>
> ➤ Timeliness addresses how quickly, when or by what date the work is produced. The most common error made in setting timeliness standards is to allow no margin for error. As with other standards, timeliness standards should be set realistically in view of other performance requirements and needs of the organization.
>
> ➤ Cost-Effectiveness addresses dollar savings to the Government or working within a budget. Standards that address cost-effectiveness should be based on specific resource levels (money, personnel, or time) that generally can be documented and measured in agencies' annual fiscal year budgets. Cost-effectiveness standards may include such aspects of performance as maintaining or

reducing unit costs, reducing the time it takes to produce a product or service, or reducing waste.

For each element, decide which of these general measurers are important to the performance of the element by asking the following questions:

➤ Is quality important? Does the stakeholder or customer care how well the work is done?
➤ Is quantity important? Does the stakeholder or customer care how many are produced?
➤ Is it important that the element be accomplished by a certain time or date?
➤ Is it important that the element be done within certain cost limits?

Specific Measures. Once you've decided which general measures are important, you can develop specific measurers. It is these specific measures that will be included in the standard. To develop specific measure(s) for each element, you must determine how you would measure the quantity, quality, timeliness, and/or cost-effectiveness of the element. If it can be measured with numbers, clearly define those numbers. If performance only can be described (i.e., observed and verified), clarify who would be the best judge to appraise the work and what factors they would look for. (The first-line supervisor is often the best person to judge performance, but there may be situations, depending on what is being measured, when a peer or the customer receiving the product or service would be the best judge.)

The following questions may help you determine specific measures. For each general measure, ask:

➤ How could [quality, quantity, timeliness, and/or cost effectiveness] be measured?
➤ Is there some number or percent that could be tracked?

If not, and the element can only be judged, ask:

➤ Who could judge that the element was done well? What factors would they look for?

Writing Standards. Once you've established the specific measures that apply to the elements, you can begin to write the standards. Before writing the Fully Successful standard, you must know the number of levels that your appraisal program uses to appraise elements. For example, if you are under an appraisal program that uses two levels to appraise elements, the Fully Successful standard would describe a single point of performance, above which is Fully Successful, and below which is Unacceptable. If, however, your appraisal program uses five levels to appraise elements, you would describe the Fully Successful standard as a range, above which is higher than Fully Successful, and below which would be Minimally Successful (or equivalent). How you write the Fully Successful standard depends on the number of levels your program uses to appraise elements.

If a specific measure for an element is numeric, for example, you would list the units to be tracked and determine the range of numbers (or the single number in a program that appraises elements at two levels) that represents Fully Successful performance. If the specific measure is descriptive, you would identify the judge, list the factors that the judge would look for, and determine what he or she would see or report that verifies that Fully Successful performance for that element had been met.

Examples. Included below are examples of elements and standards. The specific measures are in italics; the performance (or range of performance) that actually establishes the level of the standard are in boldface type.

Element: Guidance and Technical Assistance. Fully Successful Standard in an appraisal program that appraises elements at five levels (to meet this standard, all of the bullets listed must be present or occur):

➢   No more than **3–8% errors per quarter**, as determined by the supervisor.

> ➤ At least 60-80% of customers agree that the employee is willing to assist and that the information they receive is helpful.
> ➤ Employee initially responds to customer requests for assistance within at least 1-8 working hours from receipt of request.

(If this standard had been written for an appraisal program that appraised elements at only two levels, the standard would have been "no more than 8% errors per quarter," "at least 60% of customers agree," and "up to 8 working hours from receipt of request.")[5]

Another way to do this, which is the way that I prefer, is to have a formal standard at both the fully successful and far exceeds levels. In this way, people will know exactly what they need to do to receive a reward.

Looking at the development of performance standards from a slightly different perspective, the Federal Labor Relations Authority says that

generally, 5 U.S.C. § 4302 requires agencies to establish performance appraisal systems that, to the maximum extent feasible, permit the accurate evaluation of performance on the basis of objective, job-related criteria. *See, e.g., United States Dep't of Health and Human Services, Soc. Sec. Admin., Boston Region,* 48 FLRA 943, 948 (1993) (SSA, Boston). To be objective, a performance standard should be "sufficiently precise and specific as to invoke a general consensus as to its meaning and content." Id. (quoting *Wilson v. HHS,* 770 F.2d 1048, 1052 (Fed. Cir. 1985) (*Wilson*)) . . . performance standards "may be more or less objective depending upon the job measured, but must be sufficiently specific to provide a firm benchmark toward which the employee must aim her performance." *Melnick v. HUD,* 42 MSPB 93, 98 (1989). However, there is no requirement that standards must be quantitative or numerical, *see Newark Air Force Station,* 30 FLRA 616, 628 (1987), and performance standards may permit subjective judgments of an employee's supervisor, *see SSA, Boston,* 48 FLRA at 948-49.

. . . A "performance standard that provides that only one incident of poor performance will result in an unsatisfactory rating on a job element is an absolute standard." *Sullivan v. Dep't of the Navy,* 44 MSPR 646, 651-52 (1990). Although the U.S. Merit Systems Protection Board (MSPB) does not hold that absolute standards are *per se* invalid, the MSPB does hold that "their establishment will generally constitute an abuse of discretion unless death, injury, breach of security, or great monetary loss could result from a single failure to meet the performance standard."[6]

Communication and Feedback

Once you have written the standards and provided the employee with a copy of them make sure that she understands what they mean. If she has any questions, this is the best time for you to answer them. Then have her sign and date the appropriate document (usually the appraisal form) indicating that she has received them.

The next step is to monitor the employee's performance. Most government organizations mandate that there be at least one formal midyear appraisal review in addition to the annual appraisal. To me, this is insufficient. I strongly believe that employees should receive feedback much more frequently than twice a year. In my experience, monthly feedback makes the most sense. In this way, employees know exactly how they are doing and they have the opportunity to make quick adjustments when necessary. They also get to know that management is keeping an eye on them and that they have to stay on their toes. Finally, for those employees who are working like gangbusters, it is comforting and highly motivating for them to receive feedback that assures them that they are doing a great job and that their efforts have not gone unnoticed.

Keep in mind that the feedback doesn't always have to be formal; often a quick comment or note will suffice. The key is to maintain constant communication in order to prevent performance problems from getting out of hand, to motivate average employees to do better, and to reinforce excellent performance. Where possible, I advocate providing employees with monthly report cards that let them know exactly how they are doing relative to their standards and their peers. Such an approach ensures that there are no surprises and no secrets, provides employees with important and timely feedback, and documents the fact that management is truly communicating with its employees regarding performance.

Once you notice that an employee's performance is not up to par, immediately bring this to her attention, preferably in a private counseling session behind closed doors. Make sure that you clearly articulate where she is failing, try and reach agreement on the facts (i.e., which standard(s) she is not meeting, or what the numbers show), and get her point of view. Stay cool, calm, collected, and professional throughout the meeting and keep the focus on her poor performance.

If she is experiencing any on-the-job or personal problems, this would be a good time to try and address them.[7] Tell her that further action will be taken if the problems continue, but stay positive and let her know that you are there to help. Write a summary of the meeting and provide a copy to the employee. Hopefully, this will solve the problem, which is always the goal.

However, if her performance problems continue, the next step is to have another meeting with her.[8] If the employee asserts her Weingarten rights (see Chapter 6) prior to or during this meeting, I would allow her to have a union official present. While I do not believe that the employee has a formal right to union representation at this meeting, it is usually a tense time for all and the employee would probably be better served by having someone who is experienced in these types of matters present and who will represent them down the line anyway. Moreover, if you deny the request, you may have to fight an unfair labor practice (ULP) charge for denying them representation, which would be one more distraction for you. On the other hand, if you have a difficult relationship with the union, you are probably better off not inviting them to the meeting. Recognize that once you open the door and start inviting the union to the meeting, you may subject yourself to a charge of past practice if you suddenly stop inviting them.

At this meeting, you want to again identify the performance standard(s) that the employee is failing to meet, as well as possible countermeasures, and give her written counseling advising her of these deficiencies and the action that will be taken if the standards are not successfully addressed.

The counseling letter should look something like the following.

Sample Counseling Letter

(Name of Employee)
(Organization Element)

SUBJECT: Letter of Counseling

Since the beginning of your rating period (October 1,
2008), you have failed to meet your performance standard
for the critical element of Guidance and Technical
Assistance. Specifically, this element requires you to
have an error rate of no more than eight percent.
However, to date, you error rate has been 15 percent,
which is unacceptable. Copies of all of your errors are
attached as well as the formula used to compute your
error rate. If your cumulative error rate does not
improve to eight percent or better, action may be taken
to place you on a performance improvement plan.

I am more than willing to assist you at any time in
helping you improve your performance. In fact, I would
like us to meet on a weekly basis over the next month to
review your work and explore ways in which you can cut
your error rate. In addition, during this same period, I
recommend that you (1) review the errors that you made to
date in order to avoid repeating them, and (2) reread our
technical manual, especially chapters three through five,
in order to help improve your knowledge about our organization's policies.

If there are any other issues that would help you
meet your performance standards that need to be brought
to my attention, please mention them to me immediately.
Also, if there is anything else that I can do to help
you, please feel free to contact me.

_____   _____
(Signature of appropriate official)   Date

"I acknowledge receipt of this document"

_____   _____
(Signature of employee)   Date

The counseling letter lets the employee know, in no uncertain terms, that her performance is unacceptable, why it is unacceptable, and the mathematics behind that determination. Moreover, it lets her know what she needs to do to meet the minimum acceptable level. It also gives her some suggestions to follow in order to improve and it makes it clear that her supervisor will work with her in a constructive manner. Furthermore, it lets the employee know what will happen in the event that her performance does not improve to the acceptable level. This is extremely important because if you have to take the next step (i.e., a performance improvement plan, or PIP), the employee will not be caught by surprise.

It also paints a picture for anyone reviewing this case at a later date that management made a good faith effort to try and assist the employee. You want to do this for two reasons: (1) Helping the employee improve is simply the right thing to do, and (2) a third party is much more likely to sustain management's action if the record is clear that management sincerely tried to help that individual.

Going Forward

If the employee's performance improves to the acceptable level, that is great. Make sure you let her know that and congratulate her on the progress she has made. Under this scenario, everyone wins: the employee, the supervisor, her coworkers, and the organization.

However, if the employee's performance does not improve, or does not improve enough to rise to the acceptable level, then it is time to examine your options. The first thing you should be aware of is your union contract. Does it have any requirements you must follow before issuing the PIP, such as a minimum of two written counselings? If it does, then follow up the first counseling letter with a second one. If it does not, then you should carefully track the employee's performance and react accordingly.

As a general rule, I believe in placing an employee whose performance is below par on a PIP sooner rather than later. The sooner you deal with a problem directly (i.e., bring it to a head), the sooner it will be resolved one way or the other.

That having been said, I also would look at several other factors before going forward with the plan. First of all, how are the other employees in the unit doing? If everyone is doing fine and meeting his or her standards, that is usually a good indication that the employee is the problem. However, if a large number of employees are failing, I would look at the issue more deeply because I would wonder if the standards are too tough, the training is inadequate, or there is some other factor present that is causing so many employees to fail.

I would also look at the trend lines. If after receiving both an oral and a written counseling the employee's performance continues to be inadequate with little sign of improvement, I would quickly issue the PIP. However, if the employee is clearly making progress but has not quite achieved the success level, I probably would wait a little longer with the hope that the employee will eventually make it. After all, if you think the employee is going to meet the standard, I see no reason to go the more formal route, which will only cause some hard feelings along the way.

The key here is to use some judgment, but to use it wisely. Treat everyone the same way, whether you like them or not; issue PIPs to everyone who is trending in the wrong direction; and take more time for people who are trending the right way. Such an approach is fair, humane, and in the best interests of the organization.

Another issue that sometimes crops up involves employees whose performance falls just below the acceptable level. I have seen supervisors take the approach that these employees are so close to making the standard that it is not worth doing anything about them. Managers figure that all the employee has to do is put his mind to it and he will achieve the minimum level, so they do nothing. The problem with this mind-set is that these employees are watering down the performance standard as well as setting up an argument of disparate treatment if another supervisor who oversees employees under the same standard decides to do the right thing and take action.

Although it would be okay to delay giving the employee who is slightly below the standard an improvement plan, this employee still should be counseled. Moreover, if the employee continues to perform at an unacceptable level, even if he is close, management needs to eventually take action. After all, the place to draw the line is at the standard and nowhere else.

The rest of this chapter will discuss how to formally deal with an employee who is failing to meet one or more of the critical elements of his performance standards. Moreover, it will walk you through the steps you need to take in order to remove an individual whose performance does not improve to the acceptable level.

Dealing with a Poor Performer

Listed below are the basic federal requirements for dealing with an employee who is struggling to meet one or more of her critical elements.

> At any time during the performance appraisal cycle that an employee's performance is determined to be unacceptable in one or more critical elements, the agency shall notify the employee of the critical element(s) for which performance is unacceptable and inform the employee of the performance requirement(s) or standard(s) that must be attained in order to demonstrate acceptable performance in his or her position. The agency should also inform the employee that unless his or her performance in the critical element(s) improves to and is sustained at an acceptable level, the employee may be reduced in grade or removed. For each critical element in which the employee's performance is unacceptable, the agency shall afford the employee a reasonable opportunity to demonstrate acceptable performance, commensurate with the duties and responsibilities of the employee's position. As part of the employee's opportunity to demonstrate acceptable performance, the agency shall offer assistance to the employee in improving unacceptable performance.[9]

Once you have decided that it is time to place the employee on a PIP, you first should sit down with upper-level management and let them know of your intentions. This is important for a couple of reasons: (1) You want to gain their support for the potential battle down the road, and (2) you want to keep them in the loop so that in the event a complaint is filed, they will not be caught off guard.

After that is accomplished, you should meet with your human resources management (HRM) advisor and let her examine the case. Show her your evidence file and let her pick it apart so you know the strengths and weaknesses of your position. Make sure that you are aware of all the potential legal and contractual issues that may come up so you are prepared from the beginning. Finally, the advisor should look at your action in conjunction with other improvement plans that have been issued in order to ensure that you are treating your employee in a manner that is consistent with other employees in similar circumstances.

There is one other option you should discuss before going forward and that is the procedure you will follow. While most federal managers know that they can deal with poor performers by issuing a PIP and then taking action if the employee fails it (under Title 5 CFR Part 432, commonly referred to as "chapter 432"), many are not aware that they can also take a performance-based action under Title 5 CFR Part 752 (known as "chapter 752"). That is the process I discussed in Chapter 6. One of the advantages of this approach is that you do not have to issue a PIP before taking action.[10] The disadvantage is that you would have to prove your case by a preponderance of the evidence, whereas if you give the employee a PIP under chapter 432, you would only have to prove your case by substantial evidence.

If you decide to take an action under chapter 752, the action should be taken if it will "promote the efficiency of the service." Under chapter 432 the action only needs to be taken for "unacceptable performance," which is a lower threshold.[11]

Unlike chapter 432, "under Chapter 752, employees can be held to ad hoc standards, such as explicit instructions or work assignments or professional standards established for certain occupations such as physicians. In some cases, it may be more appropriate to hold employees to these ad hoc standards, as long as they are no more stringent than the established performance standards."[12] Such standards will need to be measurable so that they can accurately reflect the employee's performance. (See *Wellman v. Department of Commerce*, 10 MSPR 591 (1982).)

Also be aware that if you wind up taking an action under chapter 752, your options would include removal, suspension, or demotion, whereas under chapter 432, your options would be limited to only a removal or a demotion.[13] An action under chapter 752 could be mitigated by a third party (e.g., removal could be reduced to a suspension), whereas under chapter 432, the action can only be sustained or overturned.

For the run-of-the-mill performance-based action, you are generally better off following the chapter 432 procedures because (1) the goal is to help a person who is struggling become a productive employee, so it is a good thing to try and help him improve; (2) it lets everyone know that your performance appraisal system is meaningful and that there will be reliable consequences for poor performance; and (3) your chances of prevailing before a third party are stronger because (a) third parties, especially arbitrators, tend to be more supportive of agencies that can demonstrate that they gave an employee a formal period to improve and (b) your evidentiary burden is weaker.

On the other hand, if (1) you have someone whose performance is clearly unacceptable, (2) there is little likelihood that he will improve (e.g., he has already received plenty of training for the position he holds), (3) you can demonstrate that you already made a good faith effort to help him, (4) you have a strong case, and (5) it is important to terminate this employee as quickly as you can, then chapter 752 may be the way to go.

Interestingly, most federal agencies deal with performance almost exclusively under chapter 752, not chapter 432, which is part of the problem. For example, a 2004 *Government Executive Magazine* article reported that "In 2002, MSPB heard nearly 3,000 cases dealing with employee misconduct, but only 118 under the poor performance procedures. Over the past three years, 96 percent of disciplinary appeals to MSPB have fallen under the misconduct rubric, while only 4 percent have dealt with performance."[14]

The reason why most agencies take the chapter 752 approach is so they can fire poor performers as expeditiously as possible, which certainly makes sense. However, for the reasons described above in Dealing with a Poor Performer, it is better to use your performance management system to make it clear to employees that they will be given an opportunity to improve,[15] but if they do not, they are likely to be demoted or fired with relatively little chance of prevailing on appeal.[16] Moreover, because your success rate will also be better under such an approach, in the long term, supervisors will become much more likely to take action, which will enhance the culture of accountability that you are trying to create.

Putting it differently, if you administer your system swiftly and correctly, wherein employees know that everyone will be rewarded for excellent performance and that action will be taken against all whose performance is poor, you will begin to drive the right set of employee behaviors and management will not have to spend as much time overseeing the work of the employees.

When employees realize that management is serious about implementing its performance management system, the employees are far more likely to take corrective action before management has to get involved. That will ultimately lead to better organizational performance, which is the ultimate goal.

Because I already discussed both the procedures you should follow and the strategies you should use for chapter 752 cases in Chapter 6, I will continue to focus on how to handle a case under chapter 432.

If you are still satisfied that issuing a PIP is the right thing to do, then it is time to prepare the letter. The letter should do the following:

> Tell the employee that his work is unacceptable in one or more critical elements and that he needs to improve.

> Indicate what those critical elements are, show the employee's performance relative to them to date, and indicate why he is failing.

> Advise the employee what he has to do to improve his performance in order to retain his job.

> Remind the employee that he will also have to meet the other critical elements of his job during the opportunity period.

> Explain what efforts will be made to assist him (e.g., training, mentoring, etc.).

> State how often the supervisor will meet with him during the notice period in order to review his performance.

> Mention that if he fails to meet performance standards during the opportunity period, action will be taken to reassign, demote, or remove him.

The notice should also address any contract clauses that the agency is required to follow during the PIP. For example, I once saw an agency have a performance-based action reversed because there was no reference to trying to identify the "root cause" of the employee's performance problems. The arbitrator found for the employee because the contract required the agency to work with the employee to identify the root cause of his performance deficiencies. Had the agency discussed this issue in the PIP and then documented that it had made a reasonable attempt to address it in the minutes of the meetings between the supervisor and the employee, I am confident that the agency would have prevailed.

Listed below is a sample PIP letter. Note that this is just a guide and should be written in a manner that is consistent with your organization's policies, practices, and procedures and it should meet the requirements of your union contract, if any.

Sample Performance Improvement Letter

(Name of Employee)

(Organization Element)

SUBJECT: Performance Improvement Plan

This letter formally advises you that your performance in the critical element entitled Guidance and Technical Assistance has been unacceptable and needs to improve. Specifically, this element requires you to have an error rate of no more than eight percent. However, to date, you error rate has been 17 percent, which is unacceptable. Copies of all of your errors are attached as well as the formula used to compute your error rate. Also attached is a copy of all of your performance standards.

Since your performance has been unacceptable, I have decided to place you on a performance improvement plan (PIP). Accordingly, you will be required to have an error rate of no more than eight percent during the opportunity period and to meet all of your other critical elements as well. In essence, you will be given a formal opportunity to demonstrate that you can perform at the fully successful level with respect to the critical elements of your position. This period will begin on (insert date) and end on (insert date).

If, by the end of this period, your performance has not improved to the fully successful level, or if your performance does improve to the fully successful level but you do not maintain that level for at least one year, action may be taken to reassign, demote, or remove you. (You may have to postpone the employee's annual rating if the opportunity-to-improve period is close to the end of the annual rating period. If so, add "your annual rating for the period from [insert date] through

*[insert date] will be postponed until after you've com-
pleted this opportunity period."*

    *If the employee is due his WGI, and an acceptable
level of competence determination is required, the WGI
can be postponed until the end of the opportunity-to-
improve period.)*

    During this opportunity period, you will need to do
the following in order to meet the fully successful
level in the critical elements listed previously:

1. You must improve your ability to give accurate guidance and technical assistance.
2. You should reread the following manuals and policies
   (*insert*) in order to refresh your knowledge of the
   most important technical aspects of the job.
3. You should keep the attached job aids (*attach*) handy
   to further assist you with respect to the more complicated cases.

    You can also expect me to provide you with the
following assistance, which is designed to help you
improve to an acceptable level:

1. I will ensure that you receive a reasonable mix of
   work assignments and I will discuss the more complicated work assignments with you before you begin.
2. I will see that 100 percent of your work will be
   reviewed during the opportunity period in order to
   make certain what your accuracy rate will be.
3. I will meet with you every week to give you
   continuous feedback on your progress on each
   performance standard.
4. Every two weeks, I will give you a memo letting
   you know exactly how you are doing relative to your
   standards.
5. I am also assigning Mr(s). (*name*) to serve as a
   technical mentor to you during this period. (*Note
   that this is one of the most important parts of the
   letter. Far too many of these types of notices merely
   contain canned language that gives the impression
   that the organization is not serious about helping
   the employee.)*

If you believe that personal, medical, or other problems are contributing to your performance problems, please provide me with documentation of the problem(s). You may also contact the Employee Assistance Program (EAP) at *(insert telephone number)* or me for assistance. If you wish to provide such documentation, please contact *(add name)* in the Human Resources Office at *(insert telephone number)*. She will provide you with the information you need to submit such documentation. *(If there are one or more personal or medical issues involved, it is better to get them on the table and deal with them now.)*

During your opportunity period, I will carefully monitor your performance and, at the end, I will evaluate your work and make a decision about whether your performance during the period has reached the level required for retention in your position. Once I have made that determination, I will inform you of my decision and what additional action, if any, will be taken.

If you have any questions regarding this matter, please feel free to contact me. I will be available to respond to your questions and to help you improve your performance throughout this opportunity period.

_____   _____
(Signature of appropriate official)   Date

"I acknowledge receipt of this document"

_____   _____
(Signature of employee)   Date

The Opportunity Period

The opportunity period is the employee's chance to save her job, and so it is primarily her responsibility to step things up. The PIP should tell her what she needs to do to improve, and you should expect her to follow it as conscientiously as possible. Moreover, you should expect her to demonstrate a sense of urgency, given that her job is in jeopardy. In my experience, most people who have a sense of urgency and make a good faith effort to improve during the notice period usually do; hopefully, they rise to the acceptable level. However, if the employee merely goes about her business as if nothing has changed, that surely is not a good sign and it will tell you something about the employee's long-term goals, aspirations, and desire to remain with the organization.

Although you cannot control the employee's attitude during the opportunity period, you need to make sure that you control your own actions. You must ensure that you truly attempt to assist the employee, that you do what you say you will do in the opportunity notice, and that you document your actions. All of these seem to be relatively easy things to do, and they are. But in my experience, they are often the biggest reasons why agencies lose performance-based action cases.

Another way to think about this is to make sure that you are providing the employee with the same degree of assistance that you would like to receive if you were in the employee's shoes. This is reasonable, fair, and the right thing to do. Moreover, if you take this approach, you will be able to confidently testify that you met your legal burden of trying to assist the employee during the opportunity period.

A good way to do this is to identify the gaps between the employee's performance and the organization's expectations. Can you spot a trend in the employee's errors? Are there certain things that the employee is not doing that other, more successful employees are doing, and could you recommend these to the poor employee to boost performance? The more you can pinpoint the reasons why the employee is not succeeding and show things that can be done to improve performance, the stronger your case will be.

That having been said, there may be times where there is no apparent rhyme or reason for the employee's failure, and it may simply be due to the employee's lack of ability. If that turns out to be the case, you are still in a much better position if you can say that you analyzed the employee's deficiencies and tried to spot any trends but they simply did not exist.

A key component of the improvement plan is management's periodic meetings with the employee. Each meeting should be a dialogue with the employee, wherein both of you review his performance, go over any problems that have been identified, and discuss additional steps that can be taken to help him. The employee should always be given the chance to give his perspective on how things are going and he should be provided with the opportunity to identify any issues that need addressing. At the end of the meeting, a memorandum should be prepared that summarizes (1) his performance to date during the PIP, (2) the training and/or assistance he has received, (3) steps he needs to take to improve, and (4) the employee's perspective on things, including any requests for assistance he would like to make. In this way, if management has to take action later, the employee will see it coming and there will be no doubt that management truly tried to help him.

The following is a sample memorandum.

Sample Memo Documenting PIP Counseling Session

(Name of Employee)

(Organization Element)

SUBJECT: Documentation of Performance Improvement Plan (PIP) meeting

On December 15, 2008, we met to discuss your performance under your PIP. Also present was James Smith, your union representative. During the last two weeks, your error rate was nine percent and your cumulative error rate since the start of your PIP has improved to 10 percent. While this is good progress relative to your performance before the PIP period, it is still worse than the minimum acceptable level of eight percent. Copies of all of your errors since the beginning of the PIP are attached as well as the formula used to compute your error rate. Let me remind you again that if your cumulative error rate does not improve to eight percent or better by the end of the rating period, action will be taken to reassign, demote, or remove you.

I discussed your performance with your technical mentor, (name). He informs me that he has been meeting with you each day and that the biggest area of weakness in your knowledge is customer appeals. Accordingly, I have arranged to have our expert in this area, Mr(s). (name), provide you with a one-hour training session tomorrow at 2:00 p.m. I will also provide you with some job aids in this area, which should assist you. Last, I suggested that you take extra time to review the decisions you have been making on appeals because sometimes they have been sloppy. I provided you with several examples of sloppily prepared material during the meeting, along with suggestions on how to improve them.

At the meeting, I also provided you with the opportunity to request additional assistance and you said that none was needed.

If there are any other issues that would help you meet your performance standards that need to be brought to my attention, please mention them to me immediately. Also, if there is anything else that I can do to help you, please feel free to contact me.

The next meeting is scheduled for December 29, 2008, at 10:00 a.m.

_____   _____
(Signature of appropriate official)   Date

"I acknowledge receipt of this document"

_____   _____
(Signature of employee)   Date

The minutes of each meeting should be accurate and customized. By all means avoid using nearly the same minutes for each meeting, as that will create the impression that you are simply going through the motions in trying to help the employee.

Employee Allegations and Requests

It is possible that during one of these meetings the employee will allege that her performance problems have been caused by a physical or mental impairment. In my experience, it seems that almost every government employee who has a performance problem claims that they are handicapped in some way. Maybe they are, although it often feels that this is one more employee protection being used or misused to frustrate management.

When such an allegation is made, your first step is to determine if the employee has a disability. Request medical documentation from the employee to see if it "supports a physical or mental condition that substantially limits one or more major life activities, or (if) a record of impairment exists that substantially limits one or more major life activities."[17]

If she does have a disability, determine if she is a qualified disabled person by seeing if she "can perform essential functions with or without reasonable accommodation, there is no endangerment of health and safety of employee or coworkers and (she) otherwise meets the requirements of the position."[18] If she can show that she is a qualified individual with a disability, you will need to see what accommodation she is requesting and determine if it is reasonable. Be aware that requests to modify the performance standards of a position are not appropriate.

Agencies are usually required to grant a request for reasonable accommodation from a qualified disabled person if the requests will not cause undue hardship. Some factors to consider if you receive such a request include the cost of the request, the impact of the request, the size of the organization, and the nature of the organization.

Let me give you two examples of requests that I received during my career. The first one involved an employee who was struggling to meet his standards as a customer contact representative because he was falling asleep on the job (this was also a disciplinary issue). He demonstrated through medical documentation that he was a qualified disabled person (he had a sleep disorder) and he requested that he be allowed to walk around once an hour for five minutes at a time, while answering phone calls, in order to try and stay awake. Because the request was reasonable, and it didn't have a significant impact on our ability to meet our mission, we granted the request and he improved.

In another case, we had an employee who had severe emotional problems and requested to be reassigned to a different agency and placed in a position without any stress. Although he demonstrated that he was a qualified disabled person, we denied his request because we would have been paying the employee to work for another agency, and every job has some degree of stress associated with it. The employee eventually went out on disability retirement.

A different issue that may come up during the opportunity period involves requests for leave. With respect to annual leave and leave without pay, management generally has the discretion to approve or deny the request. Concerning sick leave, employees normally have a right to take the leave if they are legitimately ill.

As a general rule of thumb, you cannot hold employees accountable for work that is not completed due to the employee being on approved leave. In most cases, as long as the employee is not on an extended absence during the PIP, that shouldn't be a problem. For example, being absent for a week or two during a 90-day opportunity period should not have any significant impact on an employee's ability to meet a quality standard, which is usually derived from the percentage of accurate work that is completed; nor should it make much of a difference on a production standard if the measure is the average number of widgets completed *while the employee is on duty.*

On the other hand, if the employee has a timeliness standard and his extended absence adversely affects his ability to achieve that standard, then you would want to consider extending the opportunity period for two reasons: It may be the fair thing to do, and a removal could be reversed on the basis that the employee was not provided a reasonable opportunity to improve.

The key here is to first recognize that, in many cases, it is up to management to grant leave. Under most circumstances, I would not grant much time off during this period because it may hurt the employee's chances of performing acceptably and it muddies up the case if you decide to go forward with an action.

Don't be surprised if all sorts of strange things happen during the opportunity period. The employee may suddenly bring in a doctor's note blaming you for all of the stress you have caused him and claim an occupational illness, or he may suddenly fall on the job (of course, out of sight from the other employees) and claim an on-the-job injury that requires 45 days' continuation of pay. The employee may even go to his congressman and try and place political pressure on you to withdraw the PIP. Regardless of what happens, your best bet is to remain cool, not get frustrated, and simply stay the course, recognizing that desperate employees will often use the system against you. To quote boxing champion Joe Louis, "He can run but he can't hide."

Eventually, the employee will run out of options and it will be time to pay the piper. The important thing from management's perspective is to not do anything stupid (e.g., do not retaliate against the employee for exercising his rights, or do not subvert the system). To some extent, it eventually becomes a game of chess. That is, for every move the employee makes, you need to make an appropriate blocking move. If he files for workers' compensation, you should consider controverting his claim; or if his congressman writes to you on his behalf, explain to the congressman why you are taking the action and assure him that you will provide the employee with every opportunity to improve.

The more professionally you play the game, the better you will be able to stay above the fray and not make any foolish moves. Remember, the goal is not to win every battle; the goal is to win the war.

When the Opportunity Period Ends

If the employee completes the opportunity period and reaches the acceptable level, that is great. This is your best-case scenario because everyone wins, at least in the short term. I say this because the employee is not off the hook, as he is still required to meet his standards. In fact, if the employee's performance subsequently falls below the acceptable level within a year from the beginning of the PIP, he may be removed from his position without receiving another opportunity to improve.

Should the employee fail the opportunity period, then management has only three choices: (1) reassignment, (2) demotion, or (3) termination. Let's look at these three options in greater detail.

> Reassignment: This refers to placing an employee in a different position at the same grade level. Because you don't have to place an employee on a formal PIP in order to reassign him, if you have what appears to be a better fit for the employee at the same grade level, you might consider reassigning him before dealing with the headaches associated with a PIP. However, if you don't do this and the employee fails his PIP, reassignment makes sense when (1) he is an employee with a good attitude and (2) the reason(s) why he failed the last position are unlikely to cause him to fail in the next job (e.g., he may have been a poor technician and the new position does not require a significant degree of technical knowledge).

➢   Demotion: The downside of a demotion is that you are going to take an employee who is likely to be disgruntled over the loss of one or more grades and then place her in a different job. On the other hand, I have sometimes seen an employee get promoted to a job that was beyond her capability and then happily return to a lower paying job that she had successfully performed for many years. Under this scenario, the organization gets to retain an employee in a job that she has proven she can perform and the employee gets a job that she knows she can do.

➢   Removal: This makes sense when you have an employee who has a bad attitude, doesn't make a sincere effort to improve, or doesn't possess the requisite ability. Removal also makes sense when you don't have any vacancies in which the employee is likely to succeed. I would not take an employee who is unable to perform one job and then place him in a different kind of job that has similar skill sets. Odds are you will have to train the employee but will end up going through another PIP anyway. It is better to cut your losses and find a new employee.

Assuming you decide to propose the employee's removal, you should first consider the employee's status during the notice period. Because the proposed removal does not involve conduct, there is no reason to place the employee in a paid nonduty status. However, you should strongly consider whether it makes sense to retain the employee in this current position. After all, why would you want to have an employee who is clearly unacceptable at his job continue to do that same job during the notice period? If you have him performing those duties pending a decision on his status, you (1) run the risk of having him make more errors, create more problems, or even in some cases sabotage your organization; and (2) you weaken your argument, at least to some extent, that he is so unacceptable that he needs to be removed. Therefore, on many occasions, you are better off placing the employee in a nonduty status with pay pending the final outcome of the proposed removal.

I suggest that you use a proposed letter that looks similar to the one that follows.

Sample Proposed Removal Letter

(Name of Employee)

(Organization Element)

SUBJECT: Proposed Removal

1. I propose to remove you from employment with (*name of agency*) based on the following reasons:

  1. On (*insert date*) you were advised that your performance in the critical element entitled Guidance and Technical Assistance was unacceptable and needed to improve. Specifically, this element requires you to have an error rate of no more than eight percent. However, as of that date, your error rate was 17 percent, which is unacceptable. You were placed on a performance improvement plan (PIP) and given until (*insert date*) to perform at the acceptable level. However, during this period, your cumulative error rate was 11 percent, which was still unacceptable. Copies of all of your errors are attached as well as the formula used to compute your error rate. Also attached is a copy of all of your performance standards.

  During the opportunity period, you were given every opportunity to improve to the fully successful level but failed to do so. In order to assist you, I (1) ensured that you received a reasonable mix of work assignments, (2) discussed the more complicated work assignments with you before you began them, (3) ensured that 100 percent of your work was reviewed during the opportunity period, in order to make certain that your error rate was accurate, (4) met with you every week and gave you continuous feedback on your progress relative to each performance standard, (5) gave you a memo every other week letting you know exactly how you were doing relative to your standards, and (6) assigned Mr(s). (*name*) to serve as a technical mentor to you during this period. (*This paints a picture for a third party that the organization made a good faith effort to help the employee.*)

  It is my belief, given your unacceptable perform-

ance, that you are unable to successfully perform
the duties of the position you hold. Therefore,
based on your unacceptable performance in the
critical element, Guidance and Technical
Assistance, as described above, I am proposing
your removal from your current position and from
the federal service.

2. You have the right to reply to this notice orally,
   or in writing, or both orally and in writing, and
   to submit affidavits in support of your reply
   showing why this notice is inaccurate and any
   other reasons why your removal should not be
   effected. The evidence on which this notice of
   proposed action is based will be available for
   your review in the Human Resources Office, Room
   (_____). You will be allowed eight (*you could give
   more*) hours of official duty time for reviewing
   the evidence relied on to support the reason(s) in
   this notice, preparing your written reply, gathering affidavits in support of your case, and making
   a personal reply. Arrangements for the use of
   official time or requests for additional time
   should be made with me. You have the right to be
   represented in this matter (*e.g., a union official
   or an attorney*).

3. You will be given until the close of business
   (*date*) to reply to these reasons orally or in
   writing, or both orally and in writing. (*The
   employee is usually given 7 to 14 calendar days to
   respond, depending in part on whether he is covered by a negotiated agreement.*) Your written
   reply should be submitted to (*deciding official*).
   He (*the deciding official*) will receive your oral
   reply or will designate an official or officials
   to receive it.

4. If you do not understand the above reason(s) why I
   am proposing your removal, contact me, or (*name*)
   of the Human Resources Management Office (*provide
   location and phone numbers of each*) for further
   explanation.

5. The final decision to effect the action proposed
   has not been made. Mr(s). (*the deciding official*),
   who will make the final decision, will give full

> and impartial consideration to your replies if
> submitted.
>
> 6. If it is the decision of Mr(s). (*the deciding
>   official*) that you be removed, your removal will
>   be effective not fewer than 30 calendar days from
>   the day after the date of receipt of this notice.
>
> 7. You will be given a written decision as soon as
>   possible after your replies have had full consid-
>   eration, or after the close of business on (*same
>   date as in paragraph 3 above*), if you do not
>   reply.
>
> 8. You will be retained in an active duty status dur-
>   ing the advance notice period.
>
> _____   _____
> (Signature of appropriate official)   Date
>
> "I acknowledge receipt of this document"
>
> _____   _____
> (Signature of employee)   Date

The proposal letter should be given to the employee in the same manner that I described for a proposal involving a conduct case (see Chapter 6). Again, this should be handled as sensitively and professionally as possible.

The Decision to Fire

The deciding official should also follow the same basic process as described in Chapter 6. That is, (1) review the employee's written reply, if any, including the evidence she chooses to submit; (2) meet with the employee and her representative, if she chooses to make a formal reply; (3) ensure that the meeting is a constructive one and ask pertinent questions; and (4) have an HRM official present at the meeting to take notes and to help prepare a summary of the meeting.

One major difference between this type of case (under Part 432) and a conduct case (under Part 752) is that the agency will not have to defend its rationale for choosing a removal. That is because mitigation to a lower action by a third party is not possible under the law.[19] Accordingly, if the deciding official finds that the employee's performance was unacceptable, even after the employee was given an opportunity to improve, and does not see a reasonable alternative, the official should sustain the removal and be confident that a third party will not be able to impose a lesser action down the road (e.g., demoting the employee). Moreover, the official does not have to address the Douglas factors because the penalty cannot be mitigated.

As with a conduct case, at this point the deciding official should take some time to review the situation in a dispassionate manner. He should review all of the evidence and examine any applicable statutes, regulations, agency policies, labor agreements, and case law. He should also speak with his HRM advisor and the employee's supervisor(s) and consider discussing the case with the person who would represent him if the case were to go to a third party. In this way, the official will have a variety of perspectives and develop a feel for what his chances would be of prevailing on appeal.

Assuming that the deciding official determines that a removal is the appropriate action, it is time to prepare the decision letter. Below is a sample decision letter.

Sample Decision Letter

```
(Name of Employee)
(Organization Element)
(City, State, and Zip Code)

SUBJECT: Removal

1. In connection with the letter of (date) in which you
   were given advance notice of your proposed removal, I
   have decided to remove you from employment effective
   (date) based on the following reasons:

   I have found that all the instances of unacceptable
   performance specified in the proposal notice of
   (insert date) are sustained, meaning that you failed
   to achieve the fully successful standard and that
   your performance in the critical element, Guidance
   and Technical Assistance, was unacceptable. I also
   find that you were given a reasonable opportunity
```

to demonstrate acceptable performance but failed to do so. Accordingly, I find that your removal for unacceptable performance is warranted.

(*The decision should be delivered to the employee within a reasonable period of time prior to the effective date of the removal [review your agency HR manual and/or your union contract to see if a specific number of days are required]. In all cases, the employee must receive the decision letter on or before the date the action will be effective.*)

2. In reaching this decision, I carefully considered your oral and written replies (*only if submitted*) along with all of the evidence developed. (*Some organizations place a detailed analysis of the employee's arguments here. I do not think that is necessary or legally required; second, I think it would make the decision letter more complicated and less focused than it need be; and finally, remember that everything you say can and will be used against you so be very careful about what you say—in other words, never say too much.*

   A better approach would be to include a succinct memo for the record that would be included in the file. Such a memo would list the employee's arguments and the deciding official's analysis of those arguments.

   Also remember that because this action is being taken under chapter 432, a Douglas factors statement is not required.)

3. You have the right to appeal this action to the Regional Director, Merit Systems Protection Board (MSPB), (*address*). The office of the MSPB must receive your appeal no later than thirty (30) calendar days after the effective date of this removal. The board requires personal delivery during normal business hours by regular mail, facsimile (fax: (*telephone*)), or commercial overnight delivery service. A copy of the board's regulations and appeal form is attached. Petitions of appeal may be in any format, including in letter form, but must contain the information specified on the appeal form.

   (*If your labor management agreement gives the employee the right to contest the removal with an arbitrator, that should be discussed here. Note that the employee would have to decide whether to appeal the removal to either an arbitrator or the MSPB because she cannot appeal to both.*

If the employee raises a medical condition and argues that it prevented him from doing his job, this would be a good time to notify him of his option to file a request for disability retirement with the OPM. In addition, if he alleges discrimination, inform him of his right to file a complaint with the agency's Office of Equal Employment Opportunity (EEO). The employee may elect to file an appeal with the MSPB or to file a complaint with the EEO office, but he may not elect to file with both.)

4. You may ask me any questions you have about this removal and I will try and answer them for you. A further explanation of your appeal rights may be obtained by consulting the Human Resources Management Office.

_____   _____
(Signature of appropriate official)   Date

"I acknowledge receipt of this document"

_____   _____
(Signature of employee)   Date

Now that you have terminated the employee for performance, remember that there still may be work to do. As in the case of a removal for conduct, once the decision is given to the employee, it may be an appropriate time to try and reach a settlement. If the employee is amenable to a settlement wherein he resigns or agrees to retire in exchange for a clean record (assuming he is not the "employee from hell") and perhaps a small cash settlement, in most cases you should take it for the reasons cited in Chapter 6.

In Chapter 8, I will talk about what happens at a third-party hearing involving a removal. I will also show you how to prepare for such a hearing so that you will be in the best possible position to win.

8

THE HEARING

IF YOU FIRE a government employee for conduct or performance, odds are the case will never go to a hearing: "MSPB statistics show that only about 20 percent of all removals and demotions are appealed."[1] Some fired employees simply give up, others resign, and a certain number retire, either optionally or through disability.

Many cases never go to a hearing because the employees settle with the agency, in some form or another. They settle for many different reasons: They do not want to risk having a removal from the government on their permanent record; they do not want to fight the government, which has far more resources than they have; they believe their odds of prevailing before a third party are small; or they just want to get on with their lives.

For example, I once removed an employee for threatening his supervisor. He was a relatively low-level employee who had a temper and a hard time following orders. Eventually, he snapped at a superior official and threatened to harm him. We proposed his removal and placed him on administrative leave with pay pending a final agency decision. Once I decided to remove him, his representative approached me in order to try and settle the case. Because this was the first time the employee had made a threat, we decided that we would allow him to resign and we paid him some money to tide him over. We felt that this was fair because (1) we needed to send a strong message that threats were unacceptable; (2) although we felt that we could no longer employ him, we believed that he would learn his lesson and not make the same mistake in another organization; (3) a resignation would ensure that we would not be overturned by a third party; and (4) the money we paid him was far less than we would have to lay out in order to defend an appeal.

That having been said, if you have a vigorous program of accountability, you can be sure that at least some of the employees you fire will appeal their removals. They may appeal because they honestly believe the decision was wrong and they want their job back; they feel they have nothing to lose (e.g., they can retire anyway); or may simply appeal out of spite and want to make the agency jump through hoops. To some extent, the reason(s) for an appeal is irrelevant; after all, whenever an employee appeals a removal, management will have to defend its action. It is that simple.

Where Employees Can Appeal Their Removals

For the most part, federal employees who are part of a bargaining unit[2] can appeal their removals to either the U.S. Merit Systems Protection Board (MSPB) or an arbitrator,[3] but not to both.[4] Just to be clear, an arbitrator "serves as a judge who conducts a 'mini-trial,' somewhat less formally than a court trial. In most cases the arbitrator is an attorney."[5] Arbitrators are different from mediators, who try and settle disputes but have no binding authority.

Employees at the state and local levels can usually appeal their removals to a local civil commission and/or an arbitrator, depending upon their unique situation. For example, in New York state, a state employee "who is dismissed, demoted, suspended without pay, fined or reprimanded, without a remittance of his/her pre-hearing suspension without pay, may appeal either to the State Civil Service Commission or to the courts. If he/she elects to appeal to the Commission, the appeal must be filed in writing within 20 days after receipt of the written notice of the determination."[6] In Cincinnati, Ohio, "Fire and Police sworn personnel, and represented employees may appeal corrective or disciplinary action that is appealable to the Civil Service Commission, or through the grievance procedure, but not both."[7]

Let's look in more detail at the two primary bodies to which federal employees can appeal, recognizing that at the state and local levels, government employees can generally appeal to similar bodies that have the same basic sets of rules.

Merit Systems Protection Board

The MSPB is an independent, quasi-judicial agency that serves as the guardian of federal merit systems. It provides oversight of the significant actions and regulations of the Office of Personnel Management (OPM) to determine whether they are in accord with the merit system. From an employee appeals perspective, the MSPB reviews adverse actions involving suspensions of more than 14 days, demotions, and removals.

Employees usually have to file their appeals to the MSPB within 30 days of the date that the adverse action becomes effective. It must be in writing, be signed by the appellant and his representative (if he has one), and contain all of the information specified in the board's regulations. After the appeal is filed, an administrative judge (AJ) will be appointed. He will issue an acknowledgment order to both parties. The order will contain a copy of the appeal and it will direct the agency to state its reason(s) for removing the employee and to submit all documents contained in its record of the action. If there are questions relating to the timeliness, or whether the removal is within the board's jurisdiction, the order will advise the appellant to address these matters.

A discovery process, which involves notices and orders of pleadings that must be filed, will follow. One or more pre-hearing conferences will also take place to narrow and clarify the issues in the appeal and to try and settle the case if possible.

If a settlement is not reached, the hearing will take place at either an MSPB office or a location supplied by the agency. During the hearing, both parties present their cases (which include opening and closing statements), the testimony of witnesses, followed by cross-examination, and the submission of documentary evidence. At the MSPB, the admission of evidence generally follows the Federal Rules of Evidence.

After the hearing is concluded, the AJ will usually take several weeks before making his decision. The entire process takes about six months.

The initial decision of the AJ becomes the final decision of the board 35 days after the decision unless a petition for review is filed with the full board in Washington, D.C. Such a petition must be filed within 35 days after the initial decision is issued or within 30 days after the initial decision is received, whichever is later.

An appellant who has been adversely affected by a final decision of the board may obtain a review of that decision by filing a petition with the United States Court of Appeals for the Federal Circuit. However, the court's standard of review is a deferential one, requiring the federal circuit to affirm the decision unless it is "(1) arbitrary, capricious, an abuse of discretion, or otherwise not in accordance with law; (2) obtained without procedures required by law, rule, or regulation having been followed; or (3) unsupported by substantial evidence."[8]

Arbitration

Arbitration is an approach to resolving disputes using a neutral third party called the arbitrator. Typically, the arbitrator's decision is binding on both parties, although the arbitrator's decision may be appealed.

The way the process works is that once an employee receives a decision to remove him, and he decides to contest it, he has to choose to either appeal his case to the MSPB or refer it to arbitration. If he wants to go to arbitration, he first must get the approval of the local union because the union frequently has to contribute a portion of the arbitrator's fee, which can be fairly substantial.

Once invoked, the union is usually responsible for gathering a list of potential arbitrators, primarily from the Federal Mediation and Conciliation Service (FMCS). Once the list, which usually comprises seven names, is received both parties normally research the background and history of each arbitrator and determine in priority order who they are interested in working with. From there, the designated representatives of each party cross off a name at a time from the list until they are left with one name. This person then becomes the arbitrator.

The representatives then advise the arbitrator of their selection, after which the arbitrator contacts the parties and takes control of the case. From here on in, the process is relatively similar to that of the MSPB's, although it is generally less formal, less legalistic, and usually involves less discovery.

The hearings themselves are also pretty similar to the MSPB's; however, the approach is often less consistent because arbitrators are not required to follow the MSPB's rules and procedures. In a sense, every arbitration is at least somewhat different because they vary by each arbitrator's individual personality.

At the end of nearly every hearing, the arbitrator will ask both parties to file briefs summarizing their cases and explaining why the arbitrator should find for them. In reality, this is your opportunity to write the arbitrator's final decision for him. After receiving the briefs, you can expect a final decision within a month or two.

Arbitration decisions can then be appealed to the MSPB if the grievant has alleged that civil rights discrimination was involved with the action. However, the scope of the board's review of arbitrators' awards is very limited; the MSPB will only modify or set aside an arbitrator's decision if the arbitrator has erred as a matter of law in interpreting civil service law, rule, or regulation. If there is no legal error, the board will not substitute its judgment for those of the arbitrator, even if it disagrees with the decision. (See *Noel Costa v. Department of Defense*, MSPB CB-7121-00-0018-V-1, May 1, 2001.)

An arbitrator's review can also be reviewed in federal circuit court, which would use the same standard of review that they would use for decisions by the MSPB.

Now that we have looked at how each body operates, let's examine the strengths and weaknesses of each body by category, recognizing that a federal agency does not get the opportunity to choose the venue under which an appeal of a removal will be contested.

Framing the Issue

For conduct-based removals before the MSPB, the issue is whether the action will promote the efficiency of the service. With respect to performance-based removals, the issue is whether the employee's performance was unacceptable. These issues are straightforward and relatively easy to demonstrate, especially if you are familiar with the MSPB's rules, procedures, and case law. That is one of the biggest advantages from management's perspective of having a case go to the MSPB—for the most part, you go into the hearing knowing what you are dealing with.

When it comes to arbitration, things are definitely looser and less defined. For example, at the beginning of the hearing, both parties generally sit down with the arbitrator to frame the issue that the arbitrator is to decide. This can get quite sticky, especially if the issue gets framed more broadly than management would like to see. In my experience, about half the time the parties agree on the issue; when they can't agree, the arbitrator unilaterally determines what the issue is.

This may not seem like a big deal, but a poorly framed issue can create lots of problems. For instance, if the issue becomes "Did management have just cause to terminate the employee?" or "Did management have appropriate reasons for removing the employee?" management may find itself with a more difficult standard to defend, and with little chance of having either the MSPB or the courts reverse the arbitrator's decision.

Always try and frame a removal issue before an arbitrator within the narrow definitions that the MSPB uses in order to give you the best possible chance to win.

Discovery

According to the Code of Federal Regulations,

> Discovery is the process, apart from the hearing, by which a party may obtain relevant information, including the identification of potential witnesses, from another person or a party, that the other person or party has not otherwise provided. Relevant information includes information that appears reasonably calculated to lead to the discovery of admissible evidence. This information is obtained to assist the parties in preparing and presenting their cases.[9]

Discovery through the MSPB is designed to allow each party to obtain relevant information needed to prepare its case. Both parties are expected to begin and finish the discovery process with minimal board intervention.

"A party seeking discovery from another party must start the process by serving a request for discovery on the representative of the other party or the party if there is no representative. The request for discovery must state the time limit for responding, as prescribed in Sec. 1201.73(d), and must specify the time and place of the taking of the deposition, if applicable."[10] Requests for discovery could include deposing witnesses, the production of documents, items for inspecting or copying, or other requests.

The MSPB's comprehensive discovery process is generally more helpful to the appellant because he or she will be trying to gather as much information as possible in order to poke holes in your case. Accordingly, from this perspective, an MSPB appeal may be more attractive to the person you removed.

The discovery process under arbitration is generally more informal and not as legalistic. In fact, despite having handled more than a dozen arbitrations, I do not recall one case where witnesses were deposed prior to the hearing. On the other hand, an appellant can usually acquire all of the documentation she wants either by making her request through the arbitrator or by having her union representative get the documentation directly from the agency, which is required by the United States code

> to furnish to the exclusive representative involved, or its authorized representative, upon request and, to the extent not prohibited by law, data–(A) which is normally maintained by the agency in the regular course of business; (B) which is reasonably available and necessary for full and proper discussion, understanding, and negotiation of subjects within the scope of collective bargaining; and (C) which does not constitute guidance, advice, counsel, or training provided for management officials or supervisors, relating to collective bargaining."[11]

The Hearing

The MSPB hearings tend to be much more formal than arbitrations. For example, a word-for-word transcript is normally made of an MSPB hearing. I have never seen a transcript made of an arbitration hearing. The MSPB hearings are generally open to the public, whereas an arbitrator can decide to close the arbitration hearing if he or she so chooses.

The MSPB AJs tend to be stricter than arbitrators and are less likely to admit questionable evidence. For example, in MSPB cases, the basic standard for admission of evidence is relevance. There is no formal standard for arbitrators and they are more likely to accept as much evidence as possible into the record and then sift through it during the decision-making process.

In MSPB cases and arbitrations, the agency generally presents its case first and is followed by the appellant. However, where a hearing is convened on issues involving jurisdiction or timeliness, the appellant usually goes first.

Likelihood of Success

"In the nearly 25 years since the MSPB began adjudicating cases, agencies have maintained a steady win rate of about 75 percent to 80 percent," according to a 2004 article in *Government Executive Magazine*.[12] For fiscal year 2007, that percentage increased slightly to 82 percent.[13] If you look at the numbers more closely, you will find that of the total number of adverse action cases that were decided by the MSPB at the regional case level in FY2007 (2,746), 1,237, or 45 percent, were dismissed, 978 were settled, and only 531 were actually adjudicated.

To put this in perspective, remember that these numbers reflect only the adverse actions that actually went to the MSPB. This means that (1) as stated earlier, roughly 80 percent of removals never make it there; (2) of those that make it, only about 20 percent get adjudicated; and (3) in those cases management prevailed more than 80 percent of the time. The bottom line is that management's real odds of losing a removal are very low.

With respect to arbitrations, management's success rate is generally not as good as it is before the MSPB.[14] This is due to several reasons. For one thing, arbitrators are generally not as knowledgeable about the federal civil service system as MSPB AJs are, so their decisions tend to be more scattered and less consistent.

For example, the one case I lost when I was representing the government involved a nursing assistant who wheeled an elderly veteran who was suffering from dementia into a hot shower because the veteran would not be quiet. While there were no witnesses to this event, the employee confessed his actions to four different government officials and we subsequently fired him for obvious reasons. At the arbitration, the employee recanted his confession and presented a witness on his behalf who was quickly discredited. Amazingly, the arbitrator found for the employee, indicating that we did not prove our case. From my perspective, the arbitrator applied an evidence standard that was far too rigid and showed that he did not truly understand 5 USC 752. Had this matter gone before the MSPB, I feel confident that the AJ would have found for the agency.

A second reason is that arbitrators, for the most part, are not bound by MSPB case law and are not nearly as accountable as the MSPB AJs. The MSPB AJs have performance standards that measure their performance, and their decisions are all reviewable by the full board. Arbitrators have no performance standards, and their decisions are only reviewed by the full board under narrow circumstances. They are, however, subject to the FMCS Arbitration Policies and Procedures and the Code of Professional Responsibility for Arbitrators of Labor-Management Disputes. Agency complaints about arbitrators are reviewed by the FMCS and may be referred to the Arbitrator Review Board.

Because arbitrators have more freedom than the MSPB AJs and are less accountable, they tend to be more independent and less consistent as a whole. This can often work against the best interests of government agencies and can result in decisions that are puzzling at best.

The third and perhaps most important reason why management tends not to do as well in arbitration is that arbitrators are independent paid contractors. As such, they recognize that they need to be sensitive to the decisions they make if they want to stay in business. They also know that before the opposing parties decide which arbitrators to strike from the list supplied by the FMCS, the parties usually do their homework, meaning that the parties will turn to one or more of the following sources, in order to learn about each arbitrator's rulings: (1) Labor Arbitration Information System, Axon Group/LRP Publications, (2) CCH, Inc., and (3) Commerce Clearing House.

If the arbitrators constantly sustain employee removals, the unions will know that and will consider them to be pro-management. Should that happen, the unions will invariably strike them off the list and they will get very little business.[15] This is the major reason why management loses a higher proportion of removals at arbitration: simple economics.

Cost

Another major difference between the two venues is cost. The MSPB is free for both the appellant and his representative because it is a government agency funded by the taxpayer. Of course, if the appellant chooses to have a private attorney represent him, the appellant will have to pay for his services.

On the other hand, if the union agrees to refer the case to arbitration, there may very well be a cost attached. Arbitration is not cheap and the union may have to pay a considerable amount of money to bring a case before an arbitrator. The amount of the union's contribution, if any, is a negotiable item that is normally covered by the parties' labor agreement. In my experience, the parties split the cost of arbitration more often than not.

Below are the FMC's statistics[16] for the average cost of arbitration.

AVERAGE DOLLAR AMOUNTS (BASED ON ALL AWARDS)
PER DIEM
RATE... $912.99

FEE...$3,780.05

EXPENSES....................................$391.01
TOTAL
CHARGE......................................$4,171.06

AVERAGE DAYS DURATION (BASED ON ALL AWARDS)
HEARING
TIME..1.07
TRAVEL
TIME... .45
STUDY
TIME...2.43

TOTAL
TIME...3.95

As you can see, the average arbitration costs more than $4,000 and takes about four days of an arbitrator's time. However, many arbitrators charge far more than the average of $912.99 per day, especially in high-cost areas, with some charging as much as $2,500 per day. Moreover, removals tend to last longer than the average 1.07 days that is shown here because these statistics include both disciplinary actions and adverse actions. In some removals, the total cost of arbitration can easily exceed $10,000.

If both parties split the cost, it can still cost the union $5,000 or more per arbitration. Because the union is a political organization that is accountable to the bargaining unit, many of whom are dues-paying members, the union has to be judicious in deciding which cases to invest in. If it is not, it may be criticized by its membership for wasting money defending poor employees who could otherwise have their day in court at no charge to the union before the MSPB.

That is why unions tend to refer only their strongest cases and the cases that have the most political importance for them to arbitration. That is also one more reason why management does not do as well in arbitration as it does before the MSPB.

Your Representatives

Whether the case goes before the MSPB or an arbitrator, you will need to have a person represent you who is knowledgeable about the case, civil service law, and basic legal principles. These days, more often than not, an attorney represents the agency before a third party. While the representative does not have to be an attorney, there are many good reasons why using one makes sense. For one thing, an attorney is trained to make legal arguments, cross-examine witnesses, and prepare briefs. Having someone with this background can often give management an edge, especially if the appellant is represented by a union steward.

Another excellent reason for using government attorneys is that they do this kind of work all the time, so they are generally familiar with the process, the rules and regulations, the case law, and, in some cases, the person who will adjudicate your case. Because they handle so many employee cases, they can easily get up to speed and provide the agency with a vigorous defense.

However, there are several downsides to using an attorney. For example, many of them have a very heavy caseload, which often makes it difficult for them to give each case the attention it needs.

Moreover, in my experience, attorneys tend to take a relatively narrow, legalistic view of each case, and not necessarily to see things from management's perspective. Management looks at a case in the context of trying to run an organization as effectively as possible, while attorneys view a case from the prism of their legal experience and in the context of the upcoming hearing. What often happens is that the overworked attorney points out all of the holes in the case and winds up pressuring management to settle when it may not be in the organization's best interests.

Another way to handle the hearing is to have a human resources management (HRM) official represent the organization. The upside of this approach is that management's representative will be familiar with the case from the beginning; will have an intimate knowledge of civil service rules, regulations, and procedures; will not be handling many if any other concurrent hearings; and will see things more from management's perspective.

The obvious downside of this approach is that until the HRM official has gotten several hearings under her belt, she will probably not be very skilled in making arguments, cross-examining witnesses, and other important steps. When I first started representing the government as an HRM official, I tried to cross-examine a witness by asking a series of leading questions. The appellant's attorney objected to the form of my questions and those objections were immediately sustained by the EEO Administrative Law Judge (ALJ). At the time, I didn't even understand what a leading question was and the ALJ had to explain it to me, which was quite embarrassing.

That having been said, I went on to win the hearing, and in fact I successfully represented the government in 29 out of 30 hearings. Moreover, being able to represent the government at all kinds of hearings greatly broadened my perspective, as it gave me the unique opportunity to watch cases proceed from beginning to end. Ultimately, this allowed me to give much better HRM advice to the managers I was assisting and it is one of the key reasons I am able to write this book.

When you choose your representative, carefully weigh the plusses and minuses of your options before making a decision. After all, the stronger your representative, the better the chances are that you will ultimately prevail.

Another thing that you should do is provide your representative with an assistant at the hearing. There are several reasons for this: (1) It will allow the representative to concentrate on the hearing and not have to worry about the administrative issues (e.g., gathering information or making photocopies), which should be handled by the assistant; (2) it will provide management with another pair of eyes at the hearing in case the representative misses something; and (3) it will develop the assistant by providing her with valuable experience that most government employees never get.

I recommend that the assistant be either an HRM official (if you decide to have an attorney represent you) or a line manager. The advantage of having an HRM official serve as an assistant is that it will provide her with the same type of valuable experiences that helped improve my skills. It will also enable her to see how her advice was translated into action and is then viewed and interpreted by a third party. Unfortunately, these days, very few HRM employees have ever been to a third-party hearing, which has resulted in a cadre of people giving HRM advice who do not completely understand the ramifications of their advice. I strongly believe that providing an HRM specialist with such an experience will make her a much better employee and technical advisor.

The advantage of having a line manager present is that (1) he can address any technical issues that may come up because he will presumably be an expert on the work and the issues in question, and (2) it will better prepare him to deal with the unique challenges of managing employees on a day-to-day basis.

The Evidence File

I discussed the evidence file issue in Chapter 6, so I am not going to repeat the same points that I already made. That having been said, you should take your time and review the file thoroughly before sending it on to the third party who will be deciding the case.

Keep in mind that you will have only one opportunity to make a good first impression on that individual. Therefore, be sure that the file is professional, easy to read, and contains all of the requisite information. A good way to approach this is to have a table of contents at the beginning of the file that lists everything that is in there and to have each key piece of information or evidence sectioned off with a divider and listed in date order, if appropriate (e.g., decision letter, Douglas factors' statement, summary of oral reply, employee's written reply, proposed removal, and so on).

For conduct cases, take a fresh look at the file and make sure it paints the picture you are trying to convey (e.g., that the employee's conduct was so bad that removal was the appropriate penalty). To do this, it should show that (1) you met all of the procedural requirements (e.g., notice, opportunity to respond, and others), (2) the preponderance of the evidence supports the charges, (3) there is a nexus between the offense(s) and the action taken, and (4) the deciding official properly considered the Douglas factors and that removal is reasonable.

If it is a performance-based case, make sure the file shows (1) that you met all of the procedural requirements, (2) what the standards were and that the employee was aware of these requirements and failed to meet them, (3) that he was given the opportunity to improve, and (4) that he still did not achieve the minimally acceptable level. In these types of cases, one of the most important things to do is demonstrate that management made a good faith effort to help the employee, so include ample evidence to demonstrate this.

Preparing for the Hearing

In my view, there are two keys to having a removal sustained by a third party: (1) management does a quality job of removing the employee by (a) following the appropriate rules, regulations, procedures, case law, and contractual requirements, (b) addressing any mitigating circumstances that may arise, and (c) maintaining excellent documentation for its actions; and (2) management does a thorough job of preparing for the hearing. Because I have already spent a great deal of time talking about the first key point, I want to now focus on the second one, which is how the agency can best prepare itself to win the hearing.

In my experience, if management does a reasonably good job of removing an employee and still loses before a third party, it is usually due to poor preparation. By this I mean the witnesses are not properly prepared for the hearing and therefore do not come across well on the stand or its representative does not do a good job of analyzing the appellant's position before the hearing and, as a result, does not pick apart the appellant's case as well as he should. Let's look at both of these scenarios.

With respect to management's witnesses, when an agency loses, it often happens because one or more of the appellant's supervisors unintentionally wind up undermining management's case. This happens because they (1) may be unfamiliar with the basics of the case; (2) do not understand key elements of the applicable statute, the agency's procedures, important case law, or the union contract; and (3) may be unprepared to respond to cross-examination—resulting in them often putting their foot in their mouths.

Concerning the basics of the case, all management witnesses should refresh their memory regarding the facts. Before the hearing, they should review the statements they have written that were included in the evidence file (e.g., memos for the record, letters of counseling, and other items) in order to be crystal clear about what happened and what they will be testifying about. After all, it is embarrassing to both the witness and the agency if the testimony is at odds with its own written statements. Moreover, should key discrepancies be noted, its credibility will be damaged, which will make it harder for the agency to meet its burden of proof.

Another thing you should do is provide each supervisory witness with information on all of the applicable legal issues that may be raised at the hearing. Each supervisor should be familiar with the provisions of the applicable statute and regulations (5 USC 432 or 5 USC 752 and the corresponding code of federal regulations), the agency's personnel manual, any local relevant policy statements, and the union contract. As I will soon demonstrate, a relatively easy way to both attack and fluster supervisory witnesses is to question them on legal and policy issues that they are not familiar with.

The third way in which management should prepare its witnesses is by having them undergo one or more mock questioning sessions. In my experience, management representatives generally do prepare their witnesses by asking them in advance many of the same questions that they will ask them at the hearing. They then critique their responses so witnesses will answer the questions in a more succinct and forthright manner, which is a good thing.

However, management rarely puts witnesses through mock cross-examinations, which I think is absolutely crucial in preparing them for the withering questions they are likely to receive from the appellant's representative. Without this type of preparation, one or more of the witnesses may falter and weaken management's chances of prevailing. I strongly believe that every management witness, especially those who are supervisors and are likely to be questioned about technical violations of the statute, regulations, or union contract, should undergo a mock cross-examination prior to the hearing.

Let me describe a mock cross-examination that I once put a management official through. The issue involved an employee who was removed for poor performance. The person I was questioning was his immediate supervisor during the appraisal period.

Q. "Mr. Jones, was your agency's performance appraisal system approved by the Office of Personnel Management, also known as OPM?"

A. "I don't know."

Q. "Are you aware that in order to take action against an employee for poor performance, an agency's performance appraisal system first has to be approved by OPM?"

A. "No, I am not." (*He is given material that states that the OPM is required by statute to review agency performance appraisal systems before they can be implemented.*)

Q. "Since you don't know whether the OPM has approved your agency's appraisal system, you don't know if you can legally take action against my client, true?"

A. "I guess so."

Q. "Mr. Jones, during this past rating period, did you ensure that my client has an up-to-date position description, access to an up-to-date copy of the department's mission and goals, and, if applicable, the career ladder plan?"

A. "I do not recall if I did or not."

Q. "And did you initiate a dialogue with my client to discuss his duties and responsibilities in relation to the organizational unit's goals and the department's mission?"

A. "Not really."

Q. "Are you aware that this is required by the union contract?"

A. "No, I am not."

Q. "Will you please read Section 6, D of the contract." (*The employee reads it.*)

Q. "Would you agree that you did not abide by that portion of the contract?"

A. "Yes."

Q. "Would you agree that it is important to follow the union contract?"

A. "Yes."

Q. "Mr. Jones, who developed my client's performance improvement plan?"

A. "I did."

Q. "Did you develop it by yourself?"

A. "Yes."

Q. "Are you aware that the union contract requires you to develop the improvement plan in consultation with the employee and union representative?" (*He shows that part of the contract to the employee.*)

A. "Not until you showed this to me."

Q. "So again, you violated the contract."

A. "I guess so."

This is just a small snippet of what that mock questioning session was like. By only asking the supervisor a few technical questions in areas that he had not familiarized himself with, I was able to make him nervous and uncomfortable. As I continued along these lines, he became increasingly agitated, and by the time I started questioning him about the actual facts of the case, he was barely paying attention to my questions and he simply wanted the session to end.

Once it was over, we critiqued the session and he agreed that he needed to do a lot more homework. At the same time, I suggested some alternate responses that might have helped him. For example, instead of acknowledging a violation of the contract, he might have said he would have to read the entire section of the contract before concluding whether there was a violation. I also suggested that he take his time before answering a question and consider his response rather than quickly blurting out an answer.

He agreed to read all of the technical material that we had available and we subsequently put him through another mock session, wherein he showed considerable improvement. By the time the hearing came around, he was prepared for almost any line of questioning. In fact, he felt that the union's cross-examination was tame in comparison to the mock sessions that we put him through. For all intents and purposes, he aced the hearing and management prevailed, in large part because all of the management witnesses were well prepared.

As I mentioned earlier, the other area where management often falters is in developing a strategy to rebut the appellant's line of defense. In my experience, on far too many occasions, management's representative approached the hearing reasonably prepared to present his own case but ill prepared to counter the appellant's arguments. As a result, these arguments went relatively unchallenged at the hearing and gave the other side a better chance to win.

This generally happens because the representative was either too busy or too overconfident to put in the time that was needed to figure out a sound counterattack. However, without such an approach, management runs the risk of allowing the employee's arguments to go unrebutted, which can easily lead to a third party finding mitigating circumstances to reduce the penalty (in a chapter 752 case) or concluding that management did not make a good faith effort to assist the employee (in a chapter 432 case).

This is an extremely important part of management's overall strategy for the hearing and needs to happen in every case. Moreover, it is not that difficult to do because the appellant almost always lays out his arguments in his written or oral reply to the proposed removal.

Let me give you a couple of examples to show how I handled this issue. Specifically, one of our employees hurt her wrist and claimed she could not return to work due to the pain from her injury. After granting her some sick leave, we received medical evidence that indicated that she could perform light duty. Accordingly, we instructed her to return to work in order to act as a receptionist and to answer our telephones; however, she still refused, alleging that she was in too much pain. We eventually proposed her removal, although the deciding official, much to my chagrin, reduced the penalty to a 30-day suspension.

The employee then appealed her suspension to the MSPB, and she argued that she had been in too much pain to return to work. Prior to the

MSPB hearing, we learned that during her absence, she had gone to Hawaii and attended a union-sponsored conference (she was a union official, but not the president). I felt that if we could prove this, it would greatly undermine her argument that she was in too much pain to come to work.

I had one of my colleagues approach the union president and ask him for the name of the airline that the union used for its trip to Hawaii. He told my colleague that they had used American Airlines. I contacted the airline and asked them if they could send me documentation indicating that the employee in question had in fact flown to Hawaii but they indicated that this information was no longer in their system of records.

Not being one to give up easily, I decided to bring an old American Airlines envelope that I had along with my used tickets to the hearing. After the appellant testified that she was in too much pain to return to work, I was given the opportunity to cross-examine her. I brandished the envelope in front of her, let her see that it contained used tickets, and smiled. I then asked her if she had flown to Hawaii to attend a union conference during the period where she had just testified that she was in too much pain to return to work. She turned pale because she believed that I had copies of the tickets from her flight to Hawaii. She hesitated, stammered a bit, and then reluctantly admitted that she had in fact gone to the union conference. Her credibility now damaged, the MSPB sustained her suspension.

Had I not taken the extra step of trying to find a way to rebut her chief argument, we may have won anyway, but who knows for certain. The point here is that I was prepared to both present management's case as strongly as possible and I did everything I could to poke holes in the appellant's arguments. To me, that is a winning formula.

On another occasion, we removed an employee for misconduct. His primary defense was that the real reason we removed him was because he had gone through our organization's alcohol and drug rehabilitation program (as a private citizen) and that senior management was prejudiced against anyone who had used drugs—even if they had been rehabilitated. To bolster his argument, he alleged that no one else from the program had ever been hired by the organization.

Although I felt that we could easily prove the misconduct charges, I also wanted to counter his claim of organizational prejudice based on the use of drugs. Accordingly, I examined the records of people who had graduated from the program and discovered that one other graduate had also been hired by our organization and was, in fact, still working there.

I was planning to introduce this information into the record when I was informed by a more experienced member of our human resources department that there were severe penalties for disclosing the name of any individual who had gone through a drug rehabilitation program without first getting his permission. I therefore had to come up with a different way to enter this information into the record. After discussing this issue with a variety of technical experts, I came up with my strategy.

At the hearing, I asked the appellant if he knew a certain person (the name of the person who had graduated from the program and was now working for our organization). He said that he did. So I then asked him where he first met this individual. He replied that he met him in the alcohol and drug rehabilitation program. I then produced a document indicating that this individual was now an employee of our organization and reminded the appellant that he had previously stated that we had never hired anyone else from the program.

The appellant's representative immediately objected to my line of questioning and indicated that I had violated federal law by disclosing the name of an individual who had gone through a drug rehabilitation program. The MSPB judge responded by reminding the representative that I had not disclosed that the individual in question had gone through the program; the appellant had. With his primary argument having been undermined, the judge sustained the employee's removal.

While it was likely that we would have won the case had we not rebutted his argument, I placed our organization in an even stronger position to win because I was prepared for my opponent's defense.

The Hearing Itself

This is the time when all of your hard work and preparation should pay off. If you adhere to the principles contained in this section and do your homework, the odds are strongly in your favor of having a positive outcome at the hearing.

Settling the Case

Prior to the hearing or before the hearing is formally scheduled, the parties are encouraged to try and reach a settlement. In my experience, MSPB judges push particularly hard for a settlement because they generally have a heavy caseload and are under time constraints. Any time they can get the parties to settle, it is one less case that they have to adjudicate.

Arbitrators have far less incentive to settle because it generally costs them money. After all, as stated earlier, they get paid for the arbitration itself, which can last as few as one to as many as several days if not more, plus the time they take to study the case, render the decision, and write it.

Regardless of who you are before, here are some factors to consider when deciding whether to settle a removal:

1. The strength of your case: The stronger your case, the less likely you should be to settle.

2. MSPB versus arbitration: As stated earlier, you generally have a better chance of prevailing before the board.

3. The overall odds of prevailing: Anytime you go to a third party, there is always a chance you will lose, no matter how strong your case is. Moreover, if it is a chapter 752 case, the decision can be sustained but the penalty may be mitigated.

4. The cost of going forward with the hearing: Weigh the cost of the hearing versus the price of settling. The hearing will entail employees, including supervisors, being diverted away from their regular jobs. Moreover, people always talk to each other and the hearing may result in many employees being more focused on the hearing than on the work itself. If the case is before an arbitrator, the agency will almost certainly bear the cost of at least some of the arbitrator's fee, even if the agency prevails. Finally, in the event that you lose, you may also be forced to shell out back pay, attorney's fees, and more. This is why settling a case for a few thousand dollars can be very attractive.

5. The settlement itself: I was much more likely to settle a case when it did not result in the employee returning to work.

6. The message you are sending: Always analyze how the settlement will be interpreted. Even though settlements usually contain nondisclosure clauses, remember that people are involved and word usually gets

out. If the settlement results in the workforce concluding that the employee paid a serious price for her misconduct or poor perform-ance, that is a good thing. On the other hand, if the settlement is viewed as the employee getting away with murder, or that manage-ment is not supporting its supervisors, you may pay a price for that decision in the long term. Of course, if your case is very weak, you may have no choice but to settle.

If you settle the case on favorable terms, great, you are done. Make sure that someone who has expertise in this area and knows how to translate an oral agreement into words writes the settlement agreement. Also, ensure that there is a release and discharge clause similar to the following:

> In consideration of the terms of this settlement, the appellant completely releases and forever discharges the agency of and from any and all past, present or future claims, demands, obligations, actions, causes of action, rights, damages, costs, loss of services, expenses, and compensation that the appel-lant now has, or which may hereafter accrue or in any way grow out of the appellant's employment with the agency.

When you settle a case, you want to ensure that you are done once and for all with the employee—there are some people in this world who no mat-ter what you do, always seem to reappear and try to bite you in the butt. That is why you need such a release.

I remember one occasion where we removed an employee who had been a tremendous problem. She was a very poor worker, constantly created havoc, and filed complaints on almost everything under the sun. After we fired her, I sat down with her attorney and settled the case, wherein she resigned in exchange for our paying her attorney fees, which would have been a fraction of the cost of the hearing. I insisted that we include a clause wherein she agreed to never again apply for a job with another one of our facilities. I did this because I suspected that she would simply sign the agree-ment, apply elsewhere, not get selected, and then file a new round of com-plaints. She reluctantly signed the agreement.

A month or so later I found out that she did exactly that. She applied for a job with another part of our organization, was not selected, and filed an EEO complaint. She argued that the settlement agreement was not valid because I had somehow coerced her into signing it. The matter eventually went to court, wherein the judge found for the agency by concluding that our agreement was indeed valid.

Opening Statement

In my experience, the best representatives are clear and concise. They lay out management's case in a logical and easy-to-understand manner so that the judge can quickly figure out why management decided to remove the appellant. They concisely explain how management will meet its legal burdens so that the judge or arbitrator will know exactly where they are going.

An experienced representative knows that judges or arbitrators have a limited attention span, so they get to the point quickly and move on. This type of professional approach is always appreciated by a third party.

On the other hand, a common sign of an inexperienced representative is one who rambles on and on, making the same point again and again. They seem to think that if you say the same thing time after time, it will increase in value. However, the opposite is often true, because less is often more. This type of an approach will most likely annoy and frustrate the person who will be deciding your case, and that is the last thing you want to do when the stakes are so high.

Presenting Your Case

I generally recommend that management have one of its best witnesses go first, which is hopefully the proposing official. This witness should explain management's case and the rationale for the proposal. She should be able to explain and defend the charges, describe the nexus between the employee's actions and the proposed action, discuss the employee's work history and disciplinary record, address the Douglas factors, if appropriate, and generally be conversant with all of the facts of the case. Another way to think about her role is that she is the person who should be able to frame the rest of the hearing.

After she is finished, the next set of witnesses, if any, should be the people who can provide additional insight into the charges. In a conduct case, they may have overheard the employee use inappropriate language, seen him hit another employee, or observed him act in an improper fashion. In a performance case, this may have been the individual who tried to mentor the employee, or did his quality reviews.

Many, although not all, of these witnesses can be first- or second-level supervisors. They are generally your most vulnerable witnesses with respect to cross-examination (for the reasons described earlier), so management's representative needs to be aware of this and be ready to object to any inappropriate questions by the appellant's representative. However, remember that you can't prepare for every possible scenario, and some of the witnesses may get bloodied.

For example, I recall one of my witnesses, who was an assistant division chief, suddenly stated in the middle of his testimony that his comments were off the record. He said this even though everything he had just said had been tape-recorded! The judge looked at me and rolled his eyes and I cringed, knowing that my witness had just lost a lot of credibility in the judge's eyes.

Other management witnesses of mine have made different blunders, ranging from completely misinterpreting the union contract to answering the wrong question. The point here is that all of your witnesses are people, and people make mistakes.

That is why management's last witness should be its best witness, someone who can both clean up the mess that may have been created by an earlier witness and also summarize management's case as effectively as possible. After all, this is the last management witness that the judge or arbitrator will hear from, so you want them to hear from your best. This approach is akin to the strategy that the great boxer Sugar Ray Robinson used at the end of his career. He always tried to finish the last 30 seconds of a round with a flourish, figuring that this is what the judges would remember and that they would score the round in his favor.

Your last witness should be the deciding official because that is the person who made the decision to remove the employee, and he is probably your most senior and experienced employee and the most skilled at oral communication. If that is the case, this individual should be able to reiterate why the appellant was removed and wrap things up effectively.

Addressing the Appellant's Case

After management presents its case, it becomes the appellant's turn. If the case involves conduct, the appellants' representative will most likely attack management's case on one or more of the following fronts: (1) They may argue that the evidence is vague, contradictory, or involves a "he said, she said" situation, and present witnesses who have a different perspective, or (2) they will present mitigating circumstances (e.g., personal or health problems, or alcohol or drug addiction) and argue that the penalty is too severe. On rare occasions, especially involving off-duty misconduct, the appellant's representative may argue that a nexus does not exist between the charge(s) and the action taken.

If the case involves performance, the likely defense will be that (1) the standard was unclear or too difficult to achieve, or (2) management did not make a good faith effort to help the employee during the opportunity period. Occasionally, the appellant may also disagree with the facts regarding his performance during the notice period, and he might argue that he did indeed achieve the standard. However, this defense should not succeed as long as you have an appraisal system that has a reasonable degree of record-keeping and you have been keeping the employee aware of his performance throughout the notice period.

In either type of case, the employee may also raise procedural issues— for example, that the opportunity period was too short, or the time between the offense and the action taken was too long.

Regardless of the strategy, management's representative should anticipate it, especially because, for the most part, it should already have been laid out in writing as part of the appellant's initial attempt to keep his job. Once he sees his counterpart take such an approach, he should try and rebut it to the maximum extent possible by cross-examining each witness, introducing case law that supports the agency's position, or continually trying to frame the issue as simply as possible. Remember, your opponent is going to try and do the opposite—that is, throw out as much stuff as possible with the hope that some of it will stick.

Things can get a bit tricky if the appellant represents himself or has an inexperienced union official represent him. Under these circumstances, the representative can be so bad that it may be painful to watch. My only advice here is (1) to continue to focus on the case as if the representative was competent, and (2) although you want to continue to articulate your key points, don't pile on your opponent and humiliate him because, if you do, the third party may begin to feel for this person and cut him more slack than he deserves.

On occasion, something will crop up that management's representative could not possibly anticipate. When this happens, you want a representative who is resourceful and thinks quickly on his feet and doesn't simply cave in at a moment's notice.

For example, I was representing management on a case I briefly described earlier wherein an employee wheeled an elderly patient into a hot shower because the patient wouldn't be quiet. We removed the employee for misconduct and he grieved the action to an arbitrator. At the arbitration, he produced a surprise witness who testified that he saw the whole thing happen. I objected to this witness because I had no advance notice of his appearance, but the arbitrator let him testify.

The witness stated that the appellant had nothing to do with the incident and that he personally saw the patient wheel himself into the hot shower. Surprised, I didn't initially know what to do. I finally decided to question the witness in great detail until I could figure something out.

I asked him how the patient was positioned in the wheelchair, and he indicated that the patient sat straight up, held upright by a Posey belt.[17] I asked him if the belt covered the patient's arms and he said that it did. I then asked him how the patient could move the wheelchair if his arms were restrained. He said that the patient moved the wheelchair with his legs. I then asked him how the patient was able to open the door to the shower room and he indicated that the patient kicked it open with his foot. When I then pointed out that the only way to open the door was to pull it open, the witness hemmed and hawed and his credibility was destroyed. The lesson here is that I was a good representative for the government because I was well prepared yet flexible and creative enough to successfully deal with a situation that no one could have anticipated. Although I eventually lost this case, it had nothing to do with the discredited surprise witness.

Closing Arguments

This is the time to remind the judge or arbitrator why management removed the appellant. Review the case step by step, making sure that you (1) walk through each of the charges, (2) go over the key evidence for each charge, and (3) explain why you have met your burden of proof for each. Then discuss, if applicable, why there is a nexus between the charges and the action taken and follow that up with a discussion of the Douglas factors and make it clear why removal was the appropriate penalty.

After that, review the appellant's principal arguments one by one, and rebut them to the maximum extent possible. Point out weaknesses in his arguments and contradictions in the testimony of his witnesses. Wherever possible, cite case law when making your point.

At the end, give a brief summary of your case so that this is the last thing that the third party hears before making his decision. Remember, be relatively brief and concise because, after a while, third parties stop paying attention to windbags.

If a brief is then required, have your representative prepare it, but let the proposing and deciding officials, at a minimum, review it. They will offer a valuable perspective and will appreciate being kept in the loop. Think of the brief as management writing the decision for the third party because the easier you make it for him to find for you, the more likely he will.

Shortly thereafter, you will receive the decision, which will most likely be favorable, especially if you followed the principles, strategies, and tactics laid out in this book. More important, you will have accomplished something that most government managers never do: fired a poor employee. In doing this, you will have improved the efficiency of the government, gained newfound respect from senior management and employees, and increased your self-confidence as a manager, knowing that you can do what so many people think is nearly impossible.

While the appellant may appeal the decision and ultimately take you to court, odds are that you will prevail. In fact, in my 28 years in management, I never had a favorable decision reversed by a higher body.

For the moment, take a deep breath and congratulate yourself. There will be plenty of time to go back into the trenches and deal with the next problem employee.

Notes

Introduction

1. U.S. Merit Systems Protection Board, "2007 Merit Principles Survey," Washington, D.C.

2. U.S. Merit Systems Protection Board, "The Changing Federal Workplace: Employee Perspectives, A Report to the President and the Congress of the United States by the U.S. Merit Systems Protection Board," Washington, D.C., 1998.

3. Ibid.

Chapter 1

1. U.S. Office of Personnel Management, "2007 Annual Employee Survey Results," http://www.opm.gov/surveys/results/Employee/2007EmployeeSurveyResults.asp.

2. Pendleton Civil Service Reform Act (Ch. 27, 22 Stat. 403). January 16, 1883.

3. Wikipedia, the Free Encyclopedia, September 18, 2008, or Gregory Y. Titelman, *Random House Dictionary of Popular Sayings,* (New York: Random House, 1966) (first used by Senator William Learned Marcy).

4. U.S. Office of Personnel Management, "Biography of an Ideal, A History of the Civil Service," http://www.opm.gov/BiographyofAnIdeal/PUevents1789p01.htm.

5. Ibid.

6. Josiah Quincy, *Memoir of the Life of John Quincy Adams* (1858) (Michigan: Scholarly Publishing Office, University of Michigan Library, 2005), 148.

7. New World Encyclopedia, http://www.newworldencyclopedia.org/entry/Andrew_Jackson.

8. Richard Brookhiser, "The Founder of Gotham's Fortunes," http://www.city-journal.org/html/14_1_urbanities-the_founder.html, Winter 2004.

9. U.S. Office of Personnel Management, "VetGuide Appendix D: A Brief History of Veterans Preference," http://www.opm.gov/employ/veterans/html/vghist.asp.

10. Ibid.

11. U.S. Office of Personnel Management, "Biography of an Ideal, A History of the Civil Service," http://www.opm.gov/BiographyofAnIdeal/PUevents1789p01.htm.

12. Ibid.

13. Ibid.

14. Ibid.

15. See Public Law 617, Act of June 10, 1948, Public Law No. 80-617, ch. 434, 6v stat. 351

16. U.S. Office of Personnel Management, "Biography of an Ideal, A History of the Civil Service," http://www.opm.gov/BiographyofAnIdeal/PUevents1789p01.htm.

17. Ibid.

18. Ibid.

19. See *Angel G. Luevano, et al., v. Janice R. Lachance, Director, Office of Personnel Management, et al.* Consent Decree, 1981, and *Luevano v. Campbell,* 93 F.R.D. (D.D.C. 1981).

20. Tammy Flanagan, "CSRS vs. FERS," National Institute of Transition Planning, Government Executive.com, http://www.govexec.com/dailyfed/0306/033106rp.htm.

21. U.S. Office of Personnel Management, "Biography of an Ideal, A History of the Civil Service," http://www.opm.gov/BiographyofAnIdeal/PUevents1789p01.htm.

22. "A Brief History of Vice President Al Gore's National Partnership for Reinventing Government during the Administration of President Bill Clinton 1993–2001," prepared by John Kamensky, January 12, 2001, http://govinfo.library.unt.edu/npr/whoweare/historyofnpr.html.

23. In lieu of the SF-171, applicants were allowed to submit either their resume or Optional Form-612, "Optional Application for Federal Employment."

24. The other four areas were financial accountability, competitive sourcing, e-government, and budget and performance integration.

25. Social Security Online, "President's Management Agenda," http://www.ssa.gov/pma/.

26. "How Jobs Get Filled," USAJOBS.gov, http://www.usajobs.gov/infocenter/howjobsgetfilled.asp.

27. Per U.S. Census Bureau, Federal, State, and Local Governments, 2002, Census of Governments.

28. Eric Yoder, "General Federal Hiring Procedures," WPNI, *Washington Post*, Jobs/Government Careers, February 10, 2003.

29. For a more detailed description of how to get a job with the government, see Stewart Liff, *Managing Your Government Career: Success Strategies That Work* (New York: AMACOM Books, 2009).

30. OPM News Release, "OPM Initiatives Will Improve Hiring/Recruitment Process," May 8, 2008.

31. Ibid.

Chapter 2

1. A full-time equivalent employee, or FTE, represents paying someone 40 hours per week. Two part-time employees who each work 20 hours per week also equal one FTE.

2. If 40 people left throughout the year and there was at least a two-month delay to fill each vacancy, we would be saving the salary of 40 people x 8 weeks' salary, or 320 weeks of salary, which would equate to the annual salary of more than six FTE (320 / 52 = 6.15 FTE). Multiplying this by the average annual salaries of the employees we would lose would give us the precise savings.

3. It doesn't make as much sense to fill a one-of-a-kind position in advance because turnover rates are not particularly good indicators for predicting when they will become vacant. It is simply a function of the person occupying that job. Moreover, you would not have the same resources to train that person, because it is likely that relatively few individuals would even know that job. However, if you know a key position will soon become open, it is a good idea to try and backfill it a few weeks before the incumbent leaves so the new occupant can learn from his predecessor.

4. Plus the difference between the lower salaries of the trainees and the journeymen they replaced.

5. External candidates are normally rated and ranked by an HRM activity.

6. Under this scenario, you would have one person with 10 months of experience (loss in October, hire in December), one with 7 months (loss in January, hire in March), one with 4 months (loss in April, hire in June), and one with 1 month (loss in July, hire in September). Twenty-two total months divided by 4 people equals 5.5 months.

7. In the federal government, October 1 is the start of the fiscal year.

8. Under this scenario, you will not be paying one CCR for 12 months, one for 9 months, one for 6 months, and one for 3 months: $12 + 9 + 6 + 3 = 30$ months.

9. Many government agencies, including the federal government, have 26 pay periods, because they pay their employees every two weeks.

10. The VRA is a special authority by which agencies can, if they wish, appoint eligible veterans without competition to positions at any grade level through General Schedule (GS) 11 or equivalent. . . . The following veterans are eligible for such an appointment:

    – Disabled veterans

    – Veterans who served on active duty in the armed forces during a war, or in a campaign or expedition for which a campaign badge has been authorized

    – Veterans who, while serving on active duty in the armed forces, participated in a United States military operation for which an armed forces service medal was awarded

    – Recently separated veterans

11. U.S. Office of Personnel Management, "Hiring People with Disabilities,"

http://www.opm.gov/disability/PeopleWithDisabilities.asp, accessed December 24, 2008.

12. Meaning they don't have to compete with regular members of the public.

13. For additional information on these programs, see the U.S. Department of Labor's Web site entitled "VI. Federal Hiring Authorities," http://www.dol.gov/oasam/doljobs/college-guide-hire-auth.htm, accessed December 24, 2008.

14. Bureau of Human Resources, "Career Opportunities in Maine State Government," http://maine.gov/statejobs/civilsrv.htm, December 24, 2008.

15. For additional information on how veterans' preference is applied in the selection process and on selecting from the top three candidates (a.k.a. "the rule of three"), see Chapter 4: Post-Interview Review/Making Your Decision.

16. "Dot Economy Altering the Attitude toward Job Switchers," *Journal Record*, December 18, 2000, http://findarticles.com/p/articles/mi_qn4182/is_/ai_n10142518.

17. Pamcleague.org, "Veterans Hiring in the Fed Government."

18. This approach makes less sense today because a lot of the clerical work that was required when the hearing impaired were first hired has become or will become automated.

19. Unfortunately, far too many government organizations do not terminate poor employees during probation, resulting in these individuals wandering through the civil service system and reinforcing the perception that the government does not successfully deal with poor employees.

20. U.S. Department of Transportation, Federal Aviation Administration, http://www.faa.gov/about/office_org/headquarters_offices/ahr/jobs_careers/.

21. U.S. Department of Transportation, Federal Aviation Administration, http://www.faa.gov/about/office_org/headquarters_offices/ahr/jobs_careers/occupations/.

22. Ohio Hiring Management System, http://careers.ohio.gov/.

23. Stewart Liff and Pamela A. Posey, D.B.A., *Seeing Is Believing: How the New Art of Visual Management Can Boost Performance throughout Your Organization* (New York: AMACOM Books, 2004).

Chapter 3

1. Federal Jobs.net, "Qualifications Standards,"
   http://federaljobs.net/quals2.htm, accessed December 24, 2008.

2. Per job announcement number D80003, dated February 28, 2008.

   Note: "GS" refers to the General Schedule pay system, which this job is
   under. "0326" refers to the occupational series. "05/06" means that the
   job will be filled at the GS-05 level with promotion potential to the GS-
   06 level or at the GS-06 grade level.

3. Per USAJobs.gov,
   http://jobsearch.usajobs.gov/getjob.asp?JobID=69477380&brd=
   3876&AVSDM=2008%2D11%2D18+14%3A41%3A03&q=
   office+support+assistant&sort=rv&vw=d&Logo=0&ss=
   0&customapplicant=
   15513%2C15514%2C15515%2C15669%2C15523%2C15512%2C15516%
   2C45575&zip=90024&rad=5&TabNum=3&rc=2 dated December 3,
   2008.

4. Ibid.

5. "Denver, the Mile High City Jobs,"
   http://agency.governmentjobs.com/denver/default.cfm?action=
   viewjob&JobID=144819&hit_count=Yes&headerfooter=1&promo=
   0&transfer=0&WDDXJobSearchParams=%3CwddxPacket%20version
   %3D%271%2E0%27%3E%3Cheader%2F%3E%3Cdata%3E%3Cstruct
   %3E%3Cvar%20name%3D%27FIND%5FKEYWORD%27%3E
   %3Cstring%3E%3C%2Fstring%3E%3C%2Fvar%3E%3Cvar%20name
   %3D%27CATEGORYID%27%3E%3Cstring%3E%2D1%3C%2Fstring
   %3E%3C%2Fvar%3E%3Cvar%20name%3D%27TRANSFER%27%3E
   %3Cstring%3E0%3C%2Fstring%3E%3C%2Fvar%3E%3Cvar%20name
   %3D%27PROMOTIONALJOBS%27%3E%3Cstring%3E0%3C%2Fstring
   %3E%3C%2Fvar%3E%3C%2Fstruct%3E%3C%2Fdata%3E%3C
   %2FwddxPacket%3E, dated December 3, 2008.

6. Ibid.

7. U.S. Office of Personnel Management, "Qualification Standards, Policies
   and Instructions, General Policies: Application of Qualification
   Standards," http://www.opm.gov/qualifications/policy/
   ApplicationOfStds-06.asp, December 5, 2008.

8. Ibid.

9. U.S. Office of Personnel Management, "Qualifying and Ranking Applicants for Project Manager Positions," http://www.opm.gov/fedclass/PM/4_qualifying_rank_app.asp, December 28, 2008.

10. State of Georgia, "FAQ," http://www.careers.ga.gov/careersFAQ.asp, December 25, 2008.

11. USAJobs.gov, http://jobsearch.usajobs.gov/getjob.asp?JobID=77455382&AVSDM=2008%2D11%2D13+17%3A52%3A28&Logo=0&sort=rv&vw=d&brd=3876&ss=0&customapplicant=15513,15514,15515,15669,15523,15512,15516,45575&rad=100&zip=90024, December 3, 2008.

12. Ramsey County, MN, Ramsey County Job Opportunities, December 3, 2008.

13. U.S. Office of Personnel Management, "Veterans," http://www.opm.gov/veterans/html/vetguide.asp#2When.

14. Ibid.

15. Ibid.

16. Ibid.

17. Veterans Today, "News: Maryland Is Hiring Veterans Now! Veterans Jobs!" http://www.veteranstoday.com/modules.php?name=News&file=article&sid=3774, posted October 13, 2008.

18. City of Santa Clarita, "Hiring Process," http://www.santa-clarita.com/cityhall/cmo/hr/hiringprocess.asp, accessed December 22, 2008.

19. For example, they may notice that you close the door when interviewing this individual but keep it open when speaking to everyone else; or that you may spend more time with her than with other candidates.

Chapter 4

1. At that time, everyone used Standard Form 171, "Application for Federal Employment."

2. The judge told us that if we went to a hearing, he would almost certainly find against us because this was her first offense. He further threatened that if we lost the case, the employee would be reinstated as a supervisor with back pay and we would be liable for expensive attorney fees.

3. Keep in mind that I am referring to the process for hiring outside candidates, not the internal promotion actions.

4. If you are not satisfied with your possible choices, you may return the certificate and select from a different source (e.g., an internal action, a certificate at a different grade level, using a special hiring authority such as the 30 percent disabled individual authority, etc.).

5. 5 CFR 332.405.

6. U.S. Office of Personnel Management, "Vet Guide," http://www.opm.gov/veterans/html/vetguide.asp#2When, accessed December 28, 2008.

7. Section 1312 of the Human Capital Officers Act of 2002 (Title XIII of the Homeland Security Act), codified at 5 U.S.C. § 3319.

8. U.S. Office of Personnel Management, "Category Rating Fact Sheet," http://www.opm.gov/employ/category_rating/faq.asp, accessed December 28, 2008.

9. For example, in New Jersey, "The Department of Personnel operates under what is commonly known as the 'Rule of Three.' The 'Rule of Three' means that after an open competitive or promotional exam is held, the Appointing Authority may select any candidate from the top three ranks unless a veteran is in the top three ranks." New Jersey Department of Personnel, "How Veterans' Preference Works," http://www.state.nj.us/personnel/veterans/how.htm, accessed December 29, 2008.

10. New York State Department of Civil Service, "After the Examination," http://www.cs.state.ny.us/jobseeker/faq/ scorenotices.cfm#whatistheruleofthree, December 29, 2008.

11. New Jersey Department of Personnel "FAQ's Jobs/Testing," http://www.state.nj.us/personnel/FAQS/job_seekers/job.htm, accessed December 29, 2008.

12. State of Kansas, "Kansas Civil Service Jobs," http://www.da.ks.gov/ps/aaa/recruitment/videotranscript.htm, accessed December 29, 2008.

13. Ibid.

14. It is a good idea to also mention these requirements at the end of the interview, so that they do not come as a surprise once a person is selected.

Chapter 5

1. Warner Todd Huston, "Fire All Government Workers," Blogger News Network, http://www.bloggernews.net/111337, posted October 31, 2007.

2. U.S. Office of Personnel Management, "2007 Annual Employee Survey Results," http://www.opm.gov/surveys/2007EmployeeSurveyResults.asp, December 31, 2008.

3. Wikipedia, the free Encyclopedia, "The Lloyd-LaFollete Act," (The Lloyd-LaFollete Act, August 24, 1912 § 6, 37 stat. 555), http://en.wikipedia.org/wiki/Lloyd-La_Follette_Act, January 2, 2009.

4. U.S. Office of Personnel Management, "Biography of an Ideal," http://www.opm.gov/BiographyofAnIdeal/SubMain1958-1977.asp, January 1, 2009.

5. Ibid.

6. Wikipedia, the Free Encyclopedia, "Civil Service Reform Act of 1978," http://en.wikipedia.org/wiki/Civil_Service_Reform_Act_of_1978, January 2, 2009.

7. 5 CFR 1201.56(c)(1).

8. 5 CFR 1201.56(c)(2).

9. State of Delaware, "State Employee Merit Rules—Employee Accountability," http://delawarepersonnel.com/search/mrules.asp?page=Sections&ID=12.0, accessed January 3, 2009.

10. City of St. Paul, MN, "Discharge, Reduction and Suspension," http://www.stpaul.gov/index.asp?NID=2334, accessed January 3, 2009.

11. I say "for the most part" because sometimes you may do everything right in dealing with a bad employee and still be reversed by the deciding official or a third party. That is the price we pay for living in the United States, where employees have the right to appeal actions taken against them. That being said, if you follow the advice laid out in this book, you will succeed in getting rid of the overwhelming majority of bad employees. Moreover, if you lose a case, contrary to popular belief, there is nothing to prevent you from trying to remove a bad employee a second time, if circumstances permit.

12. That having been said, I was certainly not opposed to settling a case when it sent the right message and was in the best interests of the government. For example, if an employee agreed to resign, it still meant that he was not going to return to our office. This made sense in many

cases because it spared us the expense of going to a hearing and it forestalled the possibility that we could be overturned.

13. I use the word "many" here because some poor performers simply can't do the job because of a lack of ability.

14. He had been seeing a therapist for quite a while.

15. He was not under any mobility agreement.

16. A table of penalties recommends a range of penalties for a specific infraction (e.g., for a first offense of insubordination, the range might be reprimand to removal; for the second offense, suspension to removal).

17. USAJobs.com, "Career and Career Conditional Appointments," http://www.usajobs.gov/EI38.asp, accessed January 9, 2009.

Chapter 6

1. Formal investigations of employee acts of misconduct are pretty rare and usually occur when they involve more than one individual, the misconduct has a large impact on the organization, or management believes that it needs an impartial, outside body to look into the matter.

2. 5 U.S.C. 7114(a) (2) (B) covers this at the federal level. At the state and local level, *NLRB v. J. Weingarten, Inc.*, 420 U.S. 251 (1975) is applicable.

3. IBM Corp., 341 NLRB No. 148 (June 9, 2004).

4. Epilepsy Foundation of Northeast Ohio, 331 NLRB 676 (2000), enf'd in relevant part, 268 F.3d 1095 (D.C. Cir. 2001), cert. denied, 536 U.S. 904 (2002).

5. In the federal government, a disciplinary action is generally defined as an admonishment, reprimand, or suspension of 14 days or fewer. An adverse action is a demotion, suspension of more than 14 days, or a removal.

6. Unless required by a local labor agreement, a first-line supervisor can usually issue an admonishment and a higher-level one can issue a reprimand.

7. At the federal level, employees who are part of a bargaining unit can often have their cases adjudicated by an arbitrator in lieu of the MSPB (they can choose to appeal to either body but not to both). At the state and local levels, the procedures vary; although in many cases, employees

can also appeal their cases to their Civil Service Commission and/or an arbitrator.

8. MSPB, "Questions and Answers about Appeals," http://www.afge171.org/afge/MSPBappeals.pdf, accessed January 11, 2009.

9. *Johnson v. Department of the Air Force* 13 M.S.P.R. 236, 238 (1982).

10. U.S. Merit Systems Protection Board, 2007 MSPB 313, Docket No. DA-0752-07-0143-I-1, *Samuel Valenzuela, Appellant, v. Department of the Army, Agency,* December 21, 2007. Also see *Merritt v. Department of Justice,* 6 M.S.P.R. 585, 596 (1981), modified by *Kruger v. Department of Justice,* 32 M.S.P.R. 71, 75 n.2 (1987).

11. U.S. Merit Systems Protection Board, 2007 MSPB 313, Docket No. DA-0752-07-0143-I-1, *Samuel Valenzuela, Appellant, v. Department of the Army, Agency,* December 21, 2007. Also see *Davis v. Veterans Administration,* 792 F.2d 1111, 1113 (Fed. Cir. 1986); ID at 15.

12. 661 F.2d 1071 (5th Circuit), after remand, 712 F.2nd, 213 (5th Circuit, 1983).

13. 5 M.S.P.R. 280 305-306 (1981).

14. Ibid.

15. U.S. Department of the Interior, "U.S. Department of the Interior Handbook on Charges and Penalty Selection for Disciplinary and Adverse Actions Part 3. Table of Penalties," accessed January 12, 2009.

16. Ibid.

17. U.S. Merit Systems Protection Board, MSPB 313, (2007) *Valenzuela v. The Department of the Army,* Docket No. DA-0752-07-0143 I 1.

18. U.S. Department of Veterans' Affairs, "Appendix D. Table of Examples of Offenses and Penalties, Range of Penalties for Stated Offense, Instructions for Use," MP-5, Part I Chapter 752 (December 31, 1998).

19. U.S. Merit Systems Protection Board, 2008 MSPB 40, Docket No. DE-0752-05-0291-I-3, *Jack Neuman v. United States Postal Service,* March 4, 2008. Also see, e.g., George, 104 M.S.P.R. 596, ¶ 11; Martin, 103 M.S.P.R. 153, ¶ 13.

20. "U.S. Department of State Foreign Affairs Manual Volume 6—General Services," 6 FAM 1930 Page 1 of 11, 6 FAM 1930, Local Transportation.

21. *Pope v. United States Postal Serv.,* 114 F.3d 1144, 1148 (Fed. Cir. 1997); *Brook v. Corrado,* 999 F.2d 523, 526 (Fed. Cir. 1993).

22. United States Court of Appeal for the Federal Circuit, 97-345, *Janice R. Lachance, Director, Office of Personnel Management, Petitioner, v. MSPB.*

23. *Refearn v. Department of Labor,* 58 M.S.P.R. 307 (1993), 93 FMSR 5274.

24. *Hamilton v. U.S. Postal Service,* 71 M.S.P.R. 547, 555-57 (1996).

25. The above discussions on making the facts fit and violations of statutes were influenced by the U.S. Department of the Interior's "Handbook on Charges and Penalty Selection for Disciplinary and Adverse Actions," January 16, 2009. See also *Pittman v. Department of the Interior,* 60 M.S.P.R. 365, 372 (1994).

26. U.S. Merit Systems Protection Board, 2008 MSPB 40, Docket No. DE-0752-05-0291-I-3, *Jack Neuman, Appellant, v. United States Postal Service.*

27. 5 CFR 752, 752.404(b)(3).

28. Ibid.

29. Ibid.

30. A written summary of the employee's oral reply should be forwarded to the employee and his representative for comment, and once everyone agrees that it is accurate, it should be included in the evidence file.

31. Meaning she could still appeal to the MSPB if she can establish that she did not breach the last-chance agreement. However, most of the time, the board does not accept jurisdiction.

32. *Licausi v. OPM,* 350 F.3d 1359, 1363 n.1 (Fed. Cir. 2003).

Chapter 7

1. 5 C.F.R. § 430.204.

2. U.S. Office of Personnel Management, Appraisal System Approval FAQs, http://www.opm.gov/perform/faqs/sysapp.asp, accessed January 21, 2009.

3. Title 5—Administrative Personnel, Chapter I—Office of Personnel Management, Part 430_Performance Management—Table of Contents, Subpart B Performance Appraisal for General Schedule, Prevailing Rate, and Certain Other Employees, Sec. 430.203 Definitions.

4. 5 C.F.R 432.104.

5. OPM, "Developing Performance Standards," http://www.opm.gov/perform/articles/118.asp, originally published April 1998.

6. 58 FLRA No. 148, NAGE Local R5-148 v. *Department of the Air Force, Seymour Johnson Air Force Base,* July 11, 2003.

7. For example, an on-the-job problem might involve a computer setup that places an ergonomic strain on the employee. Try and get an ergonomic specialist to fix it. A personal problem might entail an addiction to drugs or alcohol. If that were to happen, your best bet would be to refer her to an appropriate counselor.

8. There is no legal requirement to give the employee a written counseling prior to placing her on a formal performance improvement plan. However, I strongly believe that good management practice dictates that you try and resolve the matter informally before taking the more formal route.

9. 5 C.F.R. 432.104.

10. However, if you take an action under Part 752 and fail to provide a notice period, that could impact upon a third party's decision as to whether to mitigate the penalty. See *Fairall v. Veterans' Administration,* 33 MSPR 33, 1987.

11. OPM, "Resource Center for Addressing and Resolving Poor Performance, "Comparison of Part 432 v. Part 752," http://www.opm.gov/er/poor/432vs752.asp, accessed February 4, 2009.

12. Ibid.

13. You could also reassign the employee, but that would not constitute an adverse action and would not be appealable.

14. Shawn Zeller, "Tipping the Scales," *Government Executive Magazine,* January 15, 2004.

15. In my experience, most people who were placed on a PIP ultimately succeeded. They would not have had this opportunity, and the organization would have lost their services, had management simply proposed their removal.

16. Since management has a lower burden to prove on performance management cases processed under chapter 432, it has a better chance of succeeding under this approach than for cases administered under chapter 752.

17. OPM, "Resource Center for Addressing and Resolving Poor Performance; Requests for Reasonable Accommodation," http://www.opm.gov/er/poor/req4accommo.asp, accessed February 2, 2009.

18. Ibid.

19. See *Lisiecki v. Merit Systems Protection Board*, 769 F.2d 1558 (Fed. Cir. 1985).

Chapter 8

1. Monica Fuertes, "Adverse Action," *Government Executive Magazine*, accessed January 1, 1999.

2. A bargaining unit is "a grouping of employees that a union represents or seeks to represent and that the FLRA finds appropriate under the criteria of § 7112 (community of interest, effective dealings, efficiency of operations) for collective bargaining purposes. Certain types of employees cannot be included in units—e.g., management officials and supervisors." "OPM Labor Relations Glossary," http://www.opm.gov/lmr/glossary/glossarya.asp#APPROPRIATE%20UNIT, February 9, 2009. Note that employees can choose to be union members but cannot choose to exclude themselves from a bargaining unit.

3. Under limited circumstances, if an employee alleges that his removal was based on discrimination, he can choose to file a complaint of discrimination with the EEOC. However, since the vast majority of removals either go to the MSPB or arbitration, I am going to limit my discussion to those two avenues.

4. If they are not part of a bargaining unit, they can only appeal to the MSPB.

5. From the Free Dictionary, by Farlex, http://legal-dictionary.thefreedictionary.com/arbitrator, accessed February 9, 2009.

6. New York State, "Department of Disciplinary Proceedings," http://www.cs.state.ny.us/pio/summaryofcslaw/summofcsl-disciplinary.cfm#appeals, February 9, 2009.

7. City of Cincinnati, "Human Resources Policies and Procedures," http://www.cincinnati-oh.gov/cityhr/downloads/cityhr_pdf4309.pdf, accessed February 9, 2009.

8. 5 U.S.C. § 7703(c).

9. 5 CFR 1201.72.

10. 5 CFR 1201.73.

11. 5 USC 7114(b)(4).

12. Shawn Zeller, "Tipping the Scales," *Government Executive Magazine,* accessed January 15, 2004.

13. Merit Systems Protection Board, "MSPB Annual Report Fiscal Year 2007," May 2008.

14. Fifty to sixty-five percent, per John Berry, PLLC, "*MSPB v. Arbitration:* Differences Affecting Your Rights," http://worklaws.com/legal_articles/pdf/mspb_arbitration.pdf, accessed March 12, 2009.

15. Of course, the same thing will be true if they frequently find for the union. Management will be the one to quickly strike them off the list.

16. Federal Mediation and Conciliation Service, Arbitration Statistics, FY 2008, http://www.fmcs.gov/internet/itemDetail.asp?categoryID=196&itemID=21837, accessed October 2008.

17. A Posey belt provides additional leverage when transferring or moving a patient, thus reducing the risk of injury to the patient or caregiver.

Index